The Radio Adventures Of Sax Rohmer's Fu Manchu

The Radio Adventures Of Sax Rohmer's Fu Manchu

by Martin Grams, Jr.

BearManor Media
2022

The Radio Adventures Of Sax Rohmer's Fu Manchu

© 2022 Martin Grams, Jr.

All rights reserved.

No portion of this publication may be reproduced, stored, and/or copied electronically (except for academic use as a source), nor transmitted in any form or by any means without the prior written permission of the publisher and/or author.

Published in the United States of America by:

BearManor Media
1317 Edgewater Dr #110
Orlando FL 32804

bearmanormedia.com

Printed in the United States.

Typesetting and layout by John Teehan

ISBN—978-1-62933-894-1

Contents

Introduction 1

The Radio Adventures Of Sax Rohmer's
　Fu Manchu 7

The Molle Mystery Theatre "Fu Manchu" 75

Index 103

About the Author 109

Introduction

"The chimes of old Big Ben, London's historic clock, ring out. A sharp rap on a door is heard. The door creaks and warns of a stealthy entrance. A girl gasps and piercingly screams. A shot is fired. The Yellow Peril Incarnate laughs terrifyingly and sends shivers through millions of listeners from coast to coast. Dr. Fu Manchu, Mastermind of Crime, is on the air!"

Dr. Fu Manchu, the Mongolian Machiavelli of fictionist Sax Rohmer, was a resourceful scoundrel. His means of torture were ingenious and varied. He treated his unwelcome guests to such entertainment as strange and terrifying reptiles and insects could afford. He was a scientific rogue and able to bend an enemy to his will by injecting a secret serum into the blood. He commanded a death-dealing electric ray with which he hoped to sweep the world. He had a daughter who was a tartar if ever there was one. The unfortunates who fell into his power compelled fear and prayer. From secret chambers to catacombs, the radio adventures of Nayland Smith and Dr. Petrie were the equivalent to *Sherlock Holmes* mysteries but with an added attraction beyond murder and robbery: lurid, exploitative, and sensational subject matter that threatened the existence of the white man.

The notorious Dr. Fu Manchu was a mad scientist, intent upon conquering the world, but was continually foiled by the British policemen Sir Denis Nayland Smith and Dr. Petrie, in thirteen novels (1913–59), by Sax Rohmer. After the bloody Boxer Rebellion

Sax Rohmer

of 1900, which was sparked by secret societies in China whose aim was to eradicate Western and Christian influence in that country, a "Yellow Peril" panic briefly spread in the West. Amongst literary fiction, the Yellow Peril was a common subject for adventure fiction, of which Rohmer's creation became the penultimate representative of the genre, created in the likeness of the villain in the novel *The Yellow Danger; or, What Might Happen in the Division of the Chinese Empire Should Estrange all European Countries* (1898), by M.P. Shiel. This is not to say Yellow Peril stories never existed prior to Rohmer's creation.

The first of the Fu Manchu novels was *The Mystery of Dr. Fu Manchu*, published in the U.S. as *The Insidious Dr. Fu Manchu*. A master poisoner and chemist, he chose to dispose of his enemies using members of other secret societies, pythons, cobras, poisonous fungi and black spiders. He found guns or explosives to be mundane. Like many blood and thunder devices of literary fiction, he remained more elusive and mysterious, seldom making an appearance. He almost always sends his minions to commit crimes for him. In a later novel, it is revealed that Dr. Fu Manchu held doctorates from multiple universities.

One of three movie posters for films produced by Paramount from 1929 to 1931, based on the Sax Rohmer novels.

In the first three novels (1913 to 1917), Sir Denis Nayland Smith and assistant Dr. Petrie (who narrates the first three just as Dr. Watson did for the Sherlock Holmes adventures) were investigative sleuths who were determined to foil the evil doctor's schemes and apprehend him. Smith served in the Indian Imperial Police as a police commissioner in Burma, who was granted a roving commission, allowing him to exercise authorities over any group that could help him with his mission. It was these first three novels that formed the majority of the stories dramatized on radio.

When Sax Rohmer revived the series in 1931, Smith was knighted for his efforts to defeat Fu Manchu, and was then an ex-Assistant Commissioner of Scotland Yard. He would later accept a position with MI6. He initially revived the series with a Hollywood agenda in mind. The first three novels provided only so much story material and when Paramount Pictures wanted to produce a third movie, following the financial success of the first two, Rohmer went to work to hash out a new story. Warner Oland reprised his role of Dr. Fu Manchu for *Daughter of the Dragon* (1931), having played the role twice previous, but now Anna May Wong was the evil doctor's daughter who proved to be equally cunning and vile. The story would be adapted into a novel, *Daughter of Fu Manchu* in the same year. When MGM wanted to produce a film with Boris Karloff as the criminal genius, Rohmer came to the rescue with *The Mask of Fu Manchu*. When Republic Pictures wanted to produce a cliffhanger serial, Rohmer provided them with *The Drums of Fu Manchu*.

Due to the popularity of the motion pictures, television renditions, comic strips, comic books and radio dramas, the character of Fu Manchu assured a steady income of royalties, while providing the mainstream public with a fictional portrayal best associated with a white man in costume who donned a Mandarin costume and pigtail and sported a Fu Manchu mustache. Today, the mainstream public is familiar with the fictional character through imagery and not the Sax Rohmer novels. Devout readers of the printed page are aware that Rohmer wrote more than just the worldwide "Yellow Peril" conspiracies. He wrote of conventional detectives such as Paul Harley, Gaston Max, Red Kerry, Morris Klaw (an occult detective), and the Crime Magnet. His first effort at reviving the Fu Manchu

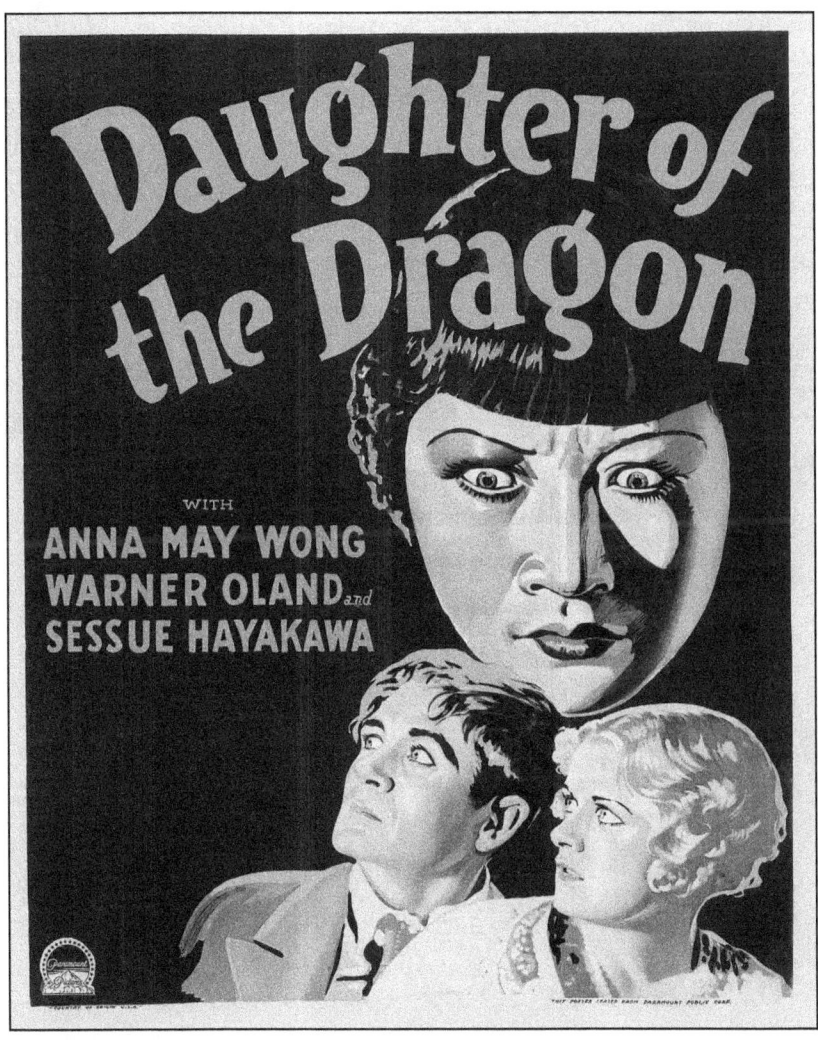

One of three movie posters for films produced by Paramount from 1929 to 1931, based on the Sax Rohmer novels.

property would ultimately be reworked as *The Emperor of America*, which would be published in both book form and be dramatized on radio in serial format.

Over the years there have been a number of works documenting and preserving the legacy of Sax Rohmer, including *Bianca in Black* (1958) by Elizabeth Sax Rohmer, *Master of Villainy: A Biography of Sax Rohmer* (1972) by Elizabeth Sax Rohmer and Cay

Van Ash with Robert Briney, *The Yellow Peril: Dr. Fu Manchu & the Rise of Chinaphobia* (2014) by Christopher Frayling, as well as additional Fu Manchu novels authorized by the Sax Rohmer estate, written by Cay Van Ash and William Patrick Maynard. In keeping with a central theme, this book will focus on the radio dramas of Fu Manchu and Sax Rohmer, debunking a number of myths and misconceptions that run rampant on the Internet.

The author of this book would like to acknowledge appreciation with the assistance of numerous people: Travis Conner, Jay Hickerson, Ted Davenport, Sammy Jones, David Lennick, William Patrick Maynard, Terry Salomonson, Karl Schadow, David Siegel, and Dr. Joe Webb.

Martin Grams, Jr.
December 2021

The Radio Adventures Of Sax Rohmer's Fu Manchu

THE INFERNAL WAR (*La Guerre Infernale*, 1908), by Pierre Giffard, is a science fiction story that depicts a World War as a fight among the empires of the white man, which distraction allows China to invade Russia, and Japan to invade the U.S. Rohmer, inspired to write adventure stories based on this premise, succeeded with sales to magazines, later culminating with the earliest of those stories fixed-up into a published novel. Literary fans will debate what published adventure tales were the inspiration for the Fu Manchu novels, with little (if any) proof, but such early publications are worthy of comparison. Regardless, Rohmer entered the literary field with songs, monologues, non-fiction and even stage plays. Among his earliest literary efforts are an occult history, *The Romance of Sorcery* (1914), and *The Quest of the Sacred Slipper* (1919), about a reporter who unearths one of Islam's holiest relics and faces off against a secret group of fanatics in modern-day.

But it was with his Oriental mysteries that today he remains strongly identified. In 1913, *The Mystery of Dr. Fu Manchu* was published in England, introducing the world at large to "the yellow peril incarnate in one man" as Rohmer described. The book would bring the author popularity and wealth. (The same novel was published in the United States as *The Insidious Dr. Fu Manchu*.)

In March of 1919, theatrical producer A.H. Woods approached Sax Rohmer about purchasing the screen rights to the Fu Manchu novels for adaptation on the silver screen. Rohmer instead chose to license the screen rights, not sell them outright, for a limited time. Woods had formed A.H. Woods Productions a year prior. By March

of 1920, Woods succeeded in licensing the screen rights for a two-year agreement, along with Rohmer's *Dope: A Story of Chinatown* (1919). *Dope* is a non-Fu Manchu novel that marks the first of what would be two novels and a number of short stories featuring the character of Chief Inspector Red Kerry. Kerry is a smart cop who uses his brain as well as his brawn to outwit and capture the criminals that threaten his city and its people. He is physically a tough man with red hair (Rohmer plays up the description more than once during the book). Because he is incorruptible and gets results, he has the backing of his superiors. In this tale, we have society and wealthy people who become ensnared in the drug culture of the early 20th century. Although there was no prohibition in the United Kingdom, they lived the same glittery life as did Americans before the Great Depression. Alcohol and drugs helped fuel the boom and the people. Kerry is trying to solve a mystery that involves a mystic/drug dealer and embroils him in a web of deceit, Chinese merchants, and passions.

As exciting as the screen adaptations would have been, Woods was unable to secure financing and the projects never met fruition.

From 1923 to 1924, the Stoll Film Company produced two series of film shorts based on the Yellow Peril stories by Sax Rohmer, a total of 23 chapter plays, following the success of *The Yellow Claw*, filmed in 1920. (Stoll was also successful with three *Adventures of Sherlock Holmes* films between 1921 and 1923.) As a result, Harry Agar Lyons became the first actor to play the role of Dr. Fu Manchu on the silver screen.

To promote his latest book, *Yellow Shadows* (published in England in 1925), the sequel to *Dope*, the second of two Inspector Red Kerry novels, Sax Rohmer went to America to promote the American printing during the spring of 1926, promoted as such: "What was the whistling death? That was the question that confronted Scotland Yard one night as the thick yellow fog rolled heavily into

> Sax Rohmer, famous English writer of the Orient, and author of the Fu Manchu stories, will give a talk from Station WEAF, New York, at 8.45 p. m., Eastern time, to-night. His subject will be a "Tale of Chinatown," which he will dramatize in a novel manner.

Newspaper clipping from the April 30, 1926 issue of *The Morning Call*, Allentown, Pennsylvania.

the mysterious room where Limehouse's richest Chinaman lay murdered. Nothing was further from the mind of Bernard Hope, sitting comfortably in his compartment of the 8:05 train from Blackwall, than thoughts of crime or death -- but when an exotically beautiful girl with an olive skin and slanting eyes stepped suddenly in, evidently badly frightened, and begged him for protection – he found himself caught in a net that nearly cost him his life."

Among Rohmer's radio interviews over WEAF in New York City was the broadcast of April 3, 1926, where the author discussed "My Experiences in the East." For 15 minutes, with only his expressive voice and an accompanying piano, Rohmer delivered his talk. On April 29, he returned to the microphone for another 15 minutes, to discuss the horrors of his "Night in Chinatown." On April 30, he returned to the same radio mike a third time to deliver "A Tale of Chinatown."

Radio scripts during the 1920s were undeveloped, improvised and often hand-written. Extant radio scripts provide no evidence of Rohmer recounting a Fu Manchu exploit, suggesting his stories were merely tales of inspiration for the *Yellow Shadows* novel. The network provided the airtime at the expense of the publisher, Doubleday, and Rohmer was provided latitude to script his talk within the required time slot.

```
9:30—Music, markets, weather.
KOIL, COUNCIL BLUFFS—238m—1260k
7:00—The Insidious Dr. Fu-Manchu.
8:00—Fatinitza.
9:00—Show Boat.
10:30—Oklahomans.
11:00—Amos 'n' Andy.
11:15—Royal Canadians.
```

Radio listing in the December 18, 1928 issue of a newspaper from Lincoln, Nebraska.

THE KOIL BROADCASTS

Very little is known about the first radio incarnation of *Fu Manchu*, broadcast from the studios of KOIL in Omaha, Nebraska, on Tuesday evenings from 7 to 7:30 p.m. Running a span of eight broadcasts, scripted by Nate Coldwell, from November 20, 1928 to January 8, 1929, the scripts were adaptations of the first novel, *The Insidious Dr. Fu Manchu*. The cast consisted of the Brandies Players, a local repertory group under the direction of Boyd Irwin. Weather elements permitting, the broadcasts were not restricted to Nebraska; they could be heard in Wisconsin, Ohio, Montana and Delaware. Based on newspaper listings, the following adventures were dramatized:

Episode #1, "The Zayat Kiss" (November 20, 1928)
Episode #2, "The Clue of the Pigtail" (November 27, 1928)
Episode #3, "Red Moat" (December 4, 1928)
Episode #4, "The Green Mist" (December 11, 1928)
Episode #5, "The Call of Siva" (December 18, 1928)
Episode #6, "The Adventure of the Marshes" (December 25, 1928)
Episode #7, "The Clue of Andaman – Second" (January 1, 1929)
Episode #8, "The Golden Flask" (January 8, 1929)

> **BEST FEATURES TONIGHT**
> FRIDAY, AUG. 30.
> 8:30 P. M.—WLW—Cincinnati—"Great Adventures," Dr. Fu Manchu.

```
WLW—CINCINNATI—428 M., 700 K. C.
  4:00 P. M.—Ukulele Lessons by Don
      Becker.
  4:15 P. M.—Woman's Radio club; Events
      Old by Mr. Did-You-Know, and
      Events New by Bob Bishow.
  4:30 P. M.—Donhallrose trio.
  5:00 P. M.—Tea Time Tunes.
  5:30 P. M.—Livestock reports from the
      Union stockyards.
  5:40 P. M.—Polly and Anna, the Glad
      Girls.
  6:00 P. M.—Memory Tunes.
  6:10 P. M.—Sport Sidelights, with Vin-
      cent Cox.
  6:25 P. M.—Baseball scores.
  6:28 P. M.—Weather announcements.
  6:30 P. M.—Dixie Circus Series (NBC).
  7:00 P. M.—Triad program (NBC).
  7:30 P. M.—Gillette program (NBC).
  8:00 P. M. — Interwoven Entertainers
      (NBC).
  8:30 P. M.—Great Moments with Great
      Adventurers, Dr. Fu Manchu.
  9:00 P. M.—Armstrong Quakers (NBC).
```

Radio schedules as they appear in *The Dayton Daily News*, August 30, 1929

THE CINCINNATI BROADCAST

The second radio incarnation was also broadcast over a regional radio station, WLW in Cincinnati, Ohio, which was heard in Akron, Dayton and surrounding territories. According to *The Columbus Dispatch*, August 30, 1929, "Dr. Fu Manchu, the creation of Sax Rohmer, novelist, will go on the ether waves with all his sinister machinations, Friday, when one of the episodes in his career is broadcast as the weekly *Great Adventure*, at 8:30 p.m., from station WLW, Cincinnati." The program was titled *Great Moments with Great Adventures*. The radio drama may have been in conjunction with the release of Paramount's latest talking picture, *The Mysterious Dr. Fu Manchu*, starring Warner Oland, which was playing at the Lyric Theater.

THE CINCINNATI STAGE SHOW

Before radio, the sinister Dr. Fu Manchu was acted out on stage by the Stuart Walker Players at the Grand Opera House. The play concerned an oriental secret society who conceived the proposition of abducting the leading mental wizards of the world and impressing them into service for the welfare of a dynasty of supermen. McKay Morris played the role of the wily Oriental

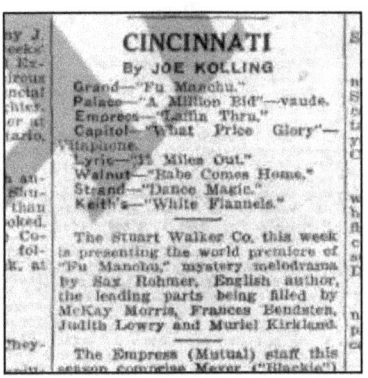
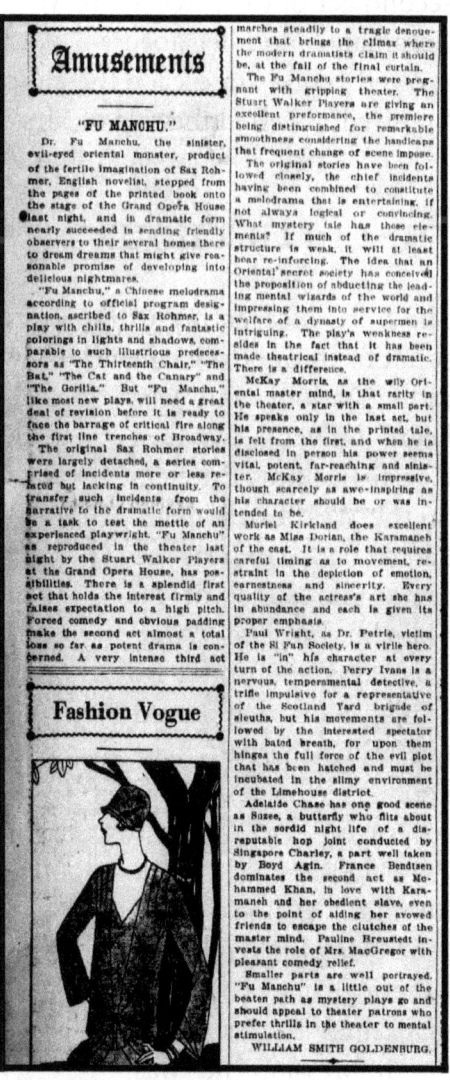

Newspaper advertisements for the Fu Manchu stage play in Cincinnati, Ohio, August 1927.

master mind, which was a small part and spoke only in the last act. Muriel Kirkland played the role of Miss Dorian, the Karamaneh of the cast. Paul Wright was Dr. Petrie, victim of the Si Fan Society. Perry Ivans was the nervous, temperamental detective of Scotland Yard. Adelaide Chase was Suzee, a butterfly who flit about in the sordid night life of a disreputable hop joint conducted by Singapore Charley, played by Boyd Agin. France Bendtsen dominated the second act of the three act play, as Mohammed Khan, in love with Karamaneh and her obedient slave, even to the point of aiding her avowed friends to escape the clutches of the master mind. Pauline Breustedt invested the role of Mrs. MacGregor with comedy relief.

THE COLLIER HOUR

The third incarnation of Fu Manchu on radio was dramatized in serial form on *The Collier Hour*, which originated from New York radio stations and was heard only on the East Coast. Luckless listeners on the West Coast never had a chance to hear the first radio serial of Fu Manchu, but *The Collier Hour* was sponsored by a magazine that could not afford coast-to-coast hookups for extensive coverage.

Although Sax Rohmer's 23 books published in England and America, and countless magazine stories, gave the impression he was writing for a generation or more, his first Fu

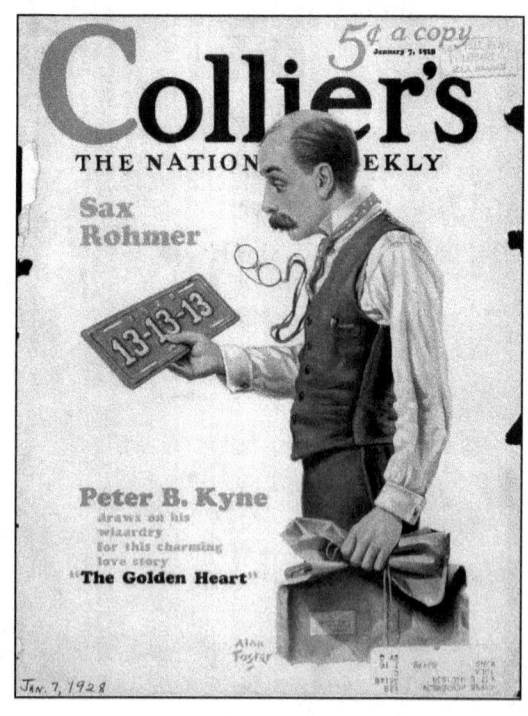

The cover of the January 7, 1928 issue of *Collier's* magazine.

Manchu stories were published concurrently in the U.S. and the U.K. from 1912 to 1913. Owing to his prolific output, he has been suspected of having lesser writers do the "padding," as did Dumas and Edgar Wallace, but Rohmer confessed in an interview: "I never have found one human being man or woman, who has been able to write a paragraph in my copy, no matter how unimportant, that did not sound like patchwork. So I am forced to do every bit of it with pencil, in longhand. Every night, invariably, I begin to work at 11 o'clock, and usually work till 3." With but the exception of until the *Collier's* publication of *Fu Manchu's Daughter*, a.k.a. *Daughter of Fu Manchu*

(1931 novel), Sax Rohmer only had three Fu Manchu novels written and published by the time the evil Oriental made his radio debut. The radio program had plenty of material to choose from, but with three novels the material was limited.

Many of Rohmer's stories were published in *Collier's* magazine, often in serial format. John B. Kennedy, managing editor of *Collier's*, appeared before the microphone in January 1927 to launch the first of what became a healthy run of weekly broadcasts, *The Collier's Hour*, providing five-minute editorials, short talks, celebrity interviews and romantic dramas that appeared in the weekly magazine. Designed to boost magazine subscriptions, the weekly hour-long program was divided into segments, each dramatizing a story or serial installment from the current issue of *Collier's* magazine. The segments were introduced by a host called The Editor, portrayed through the years by John B. Kennedy, Phil Barrison, John Erskine, and Jack Arthur. *The Collier's Hour* originated from the Times Square studios of the National Broadcasting Company in New York City.

By the summer of 1928, the fictional "Uncle Henry" was added to the program as story teller who enthralled listeners with weekly installments of baleful mysteries. Such stories also appeared in the current issues of *Collier's* at the time. Following the dramatic adaptation of E. Phillips Oppenheim's short story, "Master of Sinister House," which aired in weekly serial format beginning on the evening of October 7, 1928, it was decided to add more ominous blood and thunder stories to the program. The thrillers were, based on the overall reviews from radio critics and newspaper columnists, the highlight of the program. Perhaps no better review could best represent the critics than the one that appeared in the February 2, 1930 issue of the *Democrat and Chronicle* (Rochester, New York): "Every sort of radio feature is given here, from light opera songs to dramatizations of creepy, melodramatic mystery stories. And there is a love element, too. The program, however, would be better if it were just about 15 minutes shorter. The listener's attention tends toward strain as the program nears its close. But the program deserves the classification of one of the best on the air for general amusement, and especially creepy thrills."

Of all the serials adapted and dramatized for the radio program, three were based on Sax Rohmer novels that appeared in *Collier's* magazine:

"THE EMPEROR OF AMERICA"

(12 radio installments, November 27, 1927 to January 8, 1928, and May 13 to June 17, 1928)

(12 magazine installments, 1927: November 5, 19, December 3, 17, 24; 1928: January 7, February 11, May 19, June 2, 16, July 21, and August 18.)

It has been suggested in fanzines that *The Emperor of America* was another 12-chapter serial, broadcast on *The Collier's Hour* from November 1927 to February 1928, but no information has been found to confirm those exact dates. The serial dramatized a Fu Manchu clone with Drake Roscoe who matches wits against the master mind of Great Head Center, in what would become the prototype of an evil female Oriental known as Sumuru. Sax Rohmer's diabolical character, "The Emperor of America," was dramatized for a number of weeks, consecutive or sporadically if the February estimation can be believed, returned to the air on the evening of May 13, 1929. According to a press release: "The Emperor's temporary absence from the program was caused by the illness of his creator, who was ordered to the South of France a few weeks prior by his physician. Sax Rohmer recovered, and was again writing his tales."

"The Day the World Ended"

(12 radio installments, May 1, 1929 to July 17, 1929)
(12 magazine installments, May 4, 1929 to July 20, 1929)

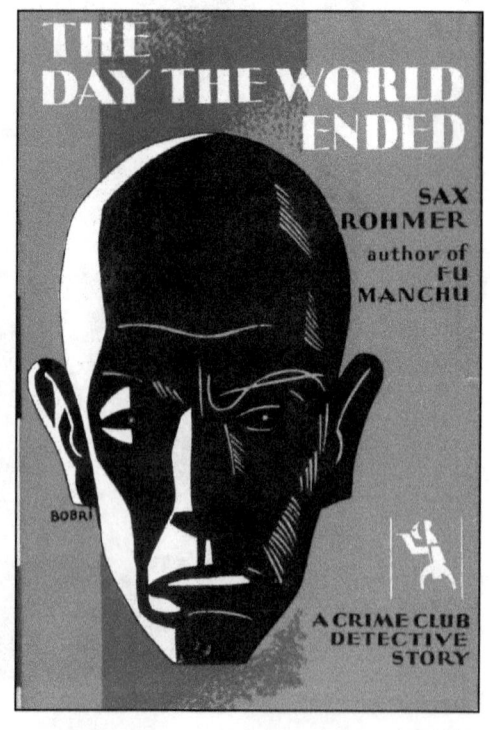

Gaston Max, Sax Rohmer's rather dapper French detective, and the greatest criminal investigator in Europe, makes his third appearance in *The Day the World Ended*. This story is closer to mainstream science fiction than any other Sax Rohmer work. It begins as a seemingly supernatural tale of vampires and strange men dressed in armor roaming castle walls. Max makes a late appearance: only to reveal that he has been present all along-in disguise. The seemingly supernatural is then revealed as the work of a strange scientist who is attempting to use his scientific achievements (including a death ray) to conquer the world.

"Fu Manchu's Daughter"
(12 installments, March 2, 1930 to May 18, 1930)
(12 magazine installments titled *Fu Manchu's Daughter*, March 8 to May 24, 1930)

Across the sands of Egypt, Nayland Smith pursues Fah Lo Suee, the deadly daughter of Fu Manchu. Possessed of all her father's subversive secrets and driven by his unquenchable thirst for power, she has pillaged the tomb of the Black Ape for the key to its ancient mysteries - and therefore leadership over all the evil cults of the East. No one can stop her - except perhaps Fu Manchu himself!

Fah Lo Suee was at that time a cultural representation of voracious Asian sexuality, later known among literature as a Dragon Lady, a charming woman who readily and easily dominated men. Sax Rohmer's novel may have been the first among literature to feature such sexual representation of the Yellow Peril, as demonstrated in the Paramount picture of the same name and later in MGM's 1932 *The Mask of Fu Manchu* (with Myrna Loy having an orgasm during the whipping scene), but many reference guides attribute the introduction of The Dragon Lady to the comic strip *Terry and the Pirates*, which premiered in 1936. On *The Collier Hour*, her sexual prowess was eliminated in place of malevolent conducts.

"Yu'an Hee See Laughs"
(12 radio installments, March 1, 1931 to May 17, 1931)
(12 magazine installments, February 28, 1931 to May 16, 1931)

"Not since the sinister Dr. Fu Manchu himself has there been a more fascinating villain than Yu'an Hee See, who moves like a dark cloud of evil through the breathless pages of this new book of mystery and adventure. Limehouse, Marseilles, the near East, the placid Mediterranean are the scenes of his murderous battle with Dawson Haigh of Scotland Yard, with the beautiful girl Haig loves as a pawn and a vast fortune of gold as the stake."

MALCOLM LAPRADE CREATED and produced *The Collier Hour*; while his brother Ernest LaPrade supplied the music scores. Colonel Davis handled direction, confessing to a newspaper reporter that he handled the assignment as amateur performances, with music and sound effects improvised during rehearsals. Radio drama was still in its infancy at the time, with radio drama evolving into the format of a stage play. Music and sound effects were added in pencil during rehearsals.

Arthur Hughes played Fu Manchu (who also doubled as "The Editor" for a majority of these broadcasts) in "Fu Manchu's Daughter." Hughes was a stage actor in New York who, along with his fellow contemporaries, supplemented income by performing on radio dramas. Hughes would later play the title role for the long-running radio soap opera, *Just Plain Bill*, and the husband of *Stella Dallas*, when the radio program premiered in 1937. Also in the cast of the Fu Manchu serial were Lenoa Beutelle, Shelagh Hayes, Hubert Rendel, and Parker Fennelly. The third episode of the series was the first broadcast from the new Times Square Studio, as a result of the studios becoming too crowded of recent. Beginning with the fourth broadcast of the serial, the actors appeared in costume on stage.

According to the files at NBC, Sax Rohmer appeared in person on March 1, 1931 (often mis-credited as May 1, 1931 in reference guides), for the premiere broadcast of "Yu'an Hee See Laughs." Rohmer's appearance was to promote the launch of the new serial and break the news to the listening audience that just weeks prior, he'd signed over the screen rights to Paramount Pictures for a third Warner Oland-Fu Manchu movie based on the serial heard on this same radio program a year earlier.

"The future of the radio is not in advertising but in culture, in opening the minds of those in the remote parts of the world and in the great cities where there are distractions of all manner of amusement," John Kennedy told 300 members of the Reading Advertisers' club at a dinner in May of 1929. "We can say that with *Collier's* magazine it has been successful. With two other magazines it has not been so helpful. Radio advertising may be a big success or a dismal failure. Everything so utterly depends on the mood of the public at the time of the broadcast… In our programs, the cardinal rule is entertainment."

Sadly, no recordings are known to exist of the Rohmer radio serials from *The Collier Hour*. Because little has been documented about the program, there exists the possibility of Fu Manchu making yet another appearance on *The Collier Hour*.

THE INSIDIOUS DR. FU MANCHU

The fourth radio incarnation of Fu Manchu came in the form of *The Insidious Dr. Fu Manchu*, a weekly radio program adapted from the first three novels, with a broadcast premiere of September 26, 1932. By this time only four Fu Manchu novels were published and Paramount maintained temporary radio rights preventing *Daughter of Fu Manchu* (the fourth novel) from being dramatized on radio without approval from the studio for publicity purposes. Rohmer was not concerned, however, as there was plenty of material in the first three to be used on the radio program. The fifth Fu Manchu novel had already been serialized in a magazine by this time, and the novel would not appear in book form until November. *The Mask of Fu Manchu*, however, was recently filmed at MGM with Boris Karloff in the lead.

Incorrectly attributed as *Fu Manchu Mysteries* because of radio logs in newspapers at the time, *The Insidious Dr. Fu Manchu* premiered on the evening of Monday, September 26, 1932, and ran a total of 31 weeks. The program was reportedly recorded in advance at WBBM in Chicago and broadcast from WGN, but there is also evidence to suggest the program was broadcast "live" from the studio of WGN in Chicago. *The Insidious Dr. Fu Manchu* was never heard on the West Coast, carried over dozens of CBS affiliates including WFAM in South Bend, Indiana; WABC in New York City; WNAC in Boston, Massachusetts; WCAO in Baltimore, Maryland; WHAS in Louisville, Kentucky; WKRC in Cincinnati, Ohio; WJSV in Washington, D.C.; WOWO in Ft. Wayne, Indiana; WFBM in Indianapolis, Indiana; WDRC in Hartford, Connecticut; WEAN in Providence, Rhode Island; KMOX in St. Louis, Missouri; KRLD in Dallas, Texas; WJAS in Pittsburgh, Pennsylvania; WCCO in Minneapolis, Minnesota; WCAU in Philadelphia, Pennsylvania; CFRB in Toronto, Canada; and CKOK in Windsor, Ontario.

September 26 to December 26, 1932
WABC in New York, 8:45 to 9:15 p.m., Eastern
WJSV in Washington D.C., 8:45 to 9:15 p.m., Eastern
WGN in Chicago, 7:45 to 8:15 p.m. Central

January 2, 1933 to April 24, 1933
WABC in New York, 8:30 to 9:00 p.m., Eastern
WJSV in Washington D.C., 8:30 to 9:00 p.m., Eastern
WGN in Chicago, 7:30 to 8:00 p.m. Central
(Beginning January 2, WGR in Buffalo was substituted
　for WKBW of the same city.)

Sponsor: Campana Corp., of Batavia, Illinois

Total Number of Radio Broadcasts: 31

September 26, 1932 – "The Zyatt Kiss"
October 2, 1932 – "The Clue of the Pigtail"
October 10, 1932 – "Redmoat" Fu Manchu will be tracked
　to a base of his nefarious operations at Redmoat Castle by
　Inspector Nailand Smith. Drugged coffee, bamboo ladders
　and secret hiding places will be in this chapter.
October 17, 1932 – "The Green Mist"
October 24, 1932 – part two

October 31, 1932 – part three. A murderous instrument which goes wrong and slays two victims allied with the Oriental.
November 7, 1932 – "The Call of Siva"
November 14, 1932 – "The Call of Siva"
November 21, 1932 – "The Call of Siva"
November 28, 1932 – "Karamaneh"
December 5, 1932 – "Karamaneh"
December 12, 1932 – "Karamaneh"
December 19, 1932 – "Andaman – Second!"
December 26, 1932 – "Andaman – Second!"
January 2, 1933 – "The Golden Mask"
January 9, 1933 – "The Spores of Death"
January 16, 1933 – [title unknown]

According to a press release, each episode was meant to be a complete drama, but it appears this was not the case. "The Green Mist," concerning a murderous instrument that slayed two victims allied with the notorious Dr. Fu Manchu, was a three-part story broadcast from October 17 to October 31, 1932.

With no recordings known to exist from this short-lived series, we can only surmise the productions based on reviews as they appeared in the columns. A radio critic for *The Indianapolis Star* reviewed: "The Fu Manchu radio presentation is a good production but too much 'allee same-ee' Sherlock Holmes, even to one of the latter's principal actors. The Sax Rohmer offering would be a great deal more effective if it were more original. Also, much would be gained if Dr. Fu Manchu could be presented as the sinister Chinese character he is supposed to be instead of the conventional, hoarse, hissing villain offered for radio consumption."

"Sound has come into its own in this half-hour," wrote Paul K. Damai, radio critic for *The Times* in Munster, Indiana. "It has at last joined the other arts of radio broadcasting. It rumbles in the valley, echoes on the mountain-side, scientifically reproduces footsteps – plain and fancy, hob-nailed and padded – and throughout it all there's that weird Fu Manchu, laughing, lip-curled, at his victims. Jack Daley's Fu is not as blood-curdling as the one heard on John B. Kennedy's magazine house [*Collier's*] a couple years ago. Charles

Warburton as the detective is the outstanding Thespian, while the heroine (with a false British accent) and Dr. Pietrie are n.s.g. And where have we heard of that detective-doctor theme before?"

"The first one was a success in creating a suspense not even commercial announcements about hand lotion could destroy," wrote Davidson Taylor, radio critic for *The Louisville Courier-Journal*. "The opening sounds, with Big Ben striking some poor defenseless London hour, are unusually effective. If a howl in the eerie night sounded once or twice like the *Lone Wolf Tribe* was on the loose, one could not mind. They are not, but just supposing that Chief Wolf Paw, Dr. Fu Manchu and Clarence of *Myrt and Marge* are one and the same person: what then? Don't let it worry you. Have yourself a good scare. Play like yellow claws were at your nape. Nothing like a good dose of adrenalin at the start of winter."

"Well institutionalized by this time and a name in goosepimple lore comparable with Sherlock Holmes himself, Fu Manchu has everything primed for an easy click on the ether waves with the possible qualifying thought that seven days is a long time between installments." *Variety* reviewed the premiere broadcast: "Fred Ibbett, the director, and most of the actors were British to ensure the program retained an English feel. Charles Warburton was imported from New York to play Nayland Smith, the super sleuth. Rohmer spoke after the first episode and did not fail to get in a puff for the advertising sponsor system as against the British non-advertising radio method."

Campana Italian Balm, through its agency, McCann-Erickson, handled the opening with expert skill; resultant volume of publicity was heavy. The advertiser paid the expenses of Sax Rohmer from Monte Carlo to Chicago and thereby provided itself with a better excuse than other new programs for crashing the newspapers. In New York, and again in Chicago, Rohmer met the press and helped make the program's start seem more like a public event than a commercial undertaking.

On Thursday, September 15, 1932, Sax Rohmer and his wife Elizabeth sailed from Southampton, having departed Monte Carlo, bound for the Big Apple. On Wednesday, September 21, the White Star line Majestic arrived in New York port. Mr. and Mrs. Rohmer stayed at the Ritz for a few days, and went sightseeing till Sunday the 25th, when Rohmer made one of his rare radio appearances for a fifteen-minute interview with CBS writer Steve Trumbull. The purpose of the interview was to publicize the radio series. Within weeks, the program brought hundreds of positive letters to CBS, and the time slot was changed to accommodate a nationwide hookup so additional stations could carry the program. Rohmer and his wife then traveled to Chicago, where they made a tour of Chicago with Police Commissioner Allman to imbibe police technique.

To promote the radio program, Sax Rohmer was interviewed by Steve Trumbull over WABC in New York City, on the afternoon of September 25, the day before the series premiere.

The opening episode, an adaptation of Rohmer's "The Zayat Kiss," varied slightly from the rest of the series, the drama lasting only twenty minutes instead of the customary 25. Introductory remarks and commercial credits usually took up the remaining five minutes, but the premiere instead featured a talk by Sax Rohmer.*

"I am deeply interested in radio and the dramatic technique," Rohmer commented, "which has been enormously developed on your [the American] side." Rohmer claimed crime was on the increase in England and attributed it largely to the influence of American crime and the fact that some American criminals had transferred their activity to London. He believed that Scotland Yard was capable enough when dealing with ordinary crimes, but frequently ineffective when faced with organized gangs. Rohmer closed his brief talk explaining to the listeners how they were lucky to have the many-sided radio of commercialism against the British specimen. Alluding to Italian Balm, the author stated he never used any skin softener himself other than whiskey, but he was sure the Campana article was the real McCoy.

Rohmer remained in Chicago for at least a week and during that time met with Fannie Butcher, literary editor of The *Chicago Tribune*, and in an interview with Rohmer, Butcher made this com-

---

* The first Fu Manchu story entitled *The Zayat Kiss* was published as a stand-alone magazine story in 1912. This and the next nine stories were combined into the novel *The Mystery of Dr. Fu Manchu* in 1913, which was titled *The Insidious Dr. Fu Manchu* when published four months later in the United States.

ment: "Such a shock as I had when I met Mr. Rohmer! I seemed to remember that Dr. Fu Manchu was one of the characters upon whom I cut my eye teeth in the mystery line, and oddly enough everyone to whom I mentioned the fact that he was arriving had the same notion. Imagine having a well set up man with the wiry English frame and the supple English youth of an indeterminate age confront one when Santa Claus was one's expectation."

NBC, meanwhile, attempted to compete with *The Orange Lantern*, the only difference being that CBS had a sponsor to pay the bill, while NBC dug into their own pocket for the lucre to feed the cast and orchestra supplying incidental (and spooky) music. When an old man stole an idol from a Chinese temple during the Boxer rebellion, his niece was kidnapped by members of a murderous cult. The hero, played by actor Jack McBryde, raced to her rescue and faced off against Wong Fu, the leader of the cult. As intriguing as this program appeals, there are no episodes of *The Orange Lantern* known to exist. The radio scripts, however, were found last year and have since been scanned into PDF files for digital backup and preservation.

Sadly, there are no recordings known to exist of *The Insidious Dr. Fu Manchu*, nor scripts found in archives to date. According to the October 1932 issue of *Broadcast Advertising*, "Universal Radio Productions of Chicago, claims to have established a new high in speed of recording programs 'off the air' last Monday night. Campana's first *Fu Manchu* program over Columbia was recorded in its entirety; then two copies of the original set of records were made, and within an hour after the program had left the air Sax Rohmer, the author, and the entire cast were listening to their own voices via Universal records."

Unlike the other Fu Manchu series, this one went all out for preparation and performances. According to a press release, the actors had to dress in full costume, and instead of the performance being acted out in a small sound studio, it was performed on stage before a live audience, recorded, and later broadcast via transcription. Sound effects were as authentic as possible. The solemn note of Big Ben and the background traffic noises of the Thames embankment were as true as could be, since they were actual recordings specially made and imported from England. Frederick George Ibbett, director of radio for the McCann-Erickson Company, the sole individual in charge of the production, would have nothing but exact sound effects. He knew his native London, having been an engineer for the BBC previous to his service with NBC and CBS.

Helen Earle and Urban Johnson supplied the sound effects. For one scene that took place during a thunderstorm, Ibbett insisted on realism so Johnson devised a new instrument, the "thunder drum." The entire hide of a cow was used in the huge device, stretched over a square frame four feet on each side. Its manufacture represented many hours of effort, but the effect was startlingly realistic.

Then there was another script in which Fu Manchu, suffering from a bullet in the brain, captured a specialist and Dr. Petrie and ordered them to perform an operation. Fu Manchu was to recover or the medical gentlemen were to be removed from the earthly scene. Ibbett again requested realism for that scene. He went to a widely known brain specialist, whom he had met socially on several occasions, and secured his professional aid in editing the script for proper surgical dialogue. More than that, he secured a real skull and the exact surgical instruments used in the operation. The conversation of the "doctors" as they performed the operation, along with the sounds of the knives, were so authentic that Ibbett later recalled how he received several letters from physicians, all asking how he accomplished the feat.

"At that time radio dramas were establishing themselves and were beginning to find favor with the music-surfeited audiences," Ibbett later recalled. "We were soon piping a good many dramatic programs to the network. You may remember *The Empire Builders*, *Rin-Tin-Tin* thrillers, *Conoco Adventures*, *Girl Reporter*, *First Nighter*..." After a couple of years at NBC, Ibbett moved across town to take a similar post with CBS, but he was there only about six months when the agency in charge of Campana's advertising called him in to supervise production on the sponsor's new *Fu Manchu* series as well as its *First Nighter* broadcasts, which he went to Hollywood to direct.

There was no music for the production. Ibbett explained that "The chance of irritating the listener, instead of creating a mood fitting the play, is too great. I prefer to omit music which might distract from the setting." The actors performed their roles in costume, so that fans could attend the stage performances and be thrilled by the spectacle of the Oriental settings. During the early productions, Ibbett drafted plans for the scenery and lighting effects, for the benefit of the audience attending the "horror chambers" of the criminal mastermind, but the cost factor could not be justified by the sponsors.

When Ibbett began a diligent search for the right actors and actresses to make Rohmer's characters spring realistically to life, he spared no expense – especially for the first broadcast. Most of the characters were British, with a wide variety of types required, and the problem of finding them in Chicago was a hard one to solve. "From all corners of the world, even far off China itself, the cast was drawn," if you can believe a 1932 CBS press release. John C. Daly (as Dr. Fu Manchu) spoke French, Chinese, Arabian, and Hindustani. Daly was born in India and his father was in the British diplomatic service. At the age of 17, Daly bolted school and went on the stage in London. Also known as Jack Daly, the radio actor played leads on *Empire Builders*, *The Adventures of Rin-Tin-Tin*, *Jack Armstrong, the All-American Boy* and as Achmed in *Tales of the Foreign Legion*. He was playing the role of Detective O'Toole in Wrigley's *Myrt and Marge* serial when he died suddenly of a pleurisy attack.

Courtesy of a press release, John Daly became somewhat of a celebrity in the trades, based on the November 13, 1933 issue of

Radio actor John C. Daly as the nefarious Fu Manchu.

The Pittsburgh Press: "Old man 'Fu Manchu' will strut his stuff on KDKA for a half hour beginning at 10:30 tonight. John C. Daly, the original Fu Manchu and Achmed Ali of the *Foreign Legion*, will star on the Princess Pageant with Doug Hope, lieutenant of the *Foreign Legion* cast." Did Daly reprise his role of Achmed or Fu Manchu during the broadcast?

Charles Warburton, for many years a favorite on the London stage, and one of the first to bring Shakespeare to radio (as Shylock in *The Merchant of Venice*), would play the role of Nayland Smith, the devil doctor's nemesis. A few years later, Warburton would seek a career in the New York radio studios and ultimately play the lead in as many as 35 dramatic programs, including the *Eno Crime Club*, *K-7: Secret Service Spy Story* and the title role of *Sherlock Holmes*. Oddly enough, although Warburton was signed to play roles in these shows, one Sherlock Holmes radio expert insists that Warburton did not act in any Holmes radio plays, but with so many radio incarnations of the Holmes character, and so little recordings existing in recorded form (compared to the thousands broadcast), it still remains a possibility that Warburton did play a few roles in the *Sherlock Holmes* broadcasts.

Norman Macdonald, who played the role of Burboyne, was a Cambridge man and was on the London stage with Sir Henry Irving and Richard Mansfield. Macdonald was brought to the radio microphone to play the minor role of Burboyne, solely for the premiere broadcast. Bob White, who played Smith's "Watson," Dr. Petrie, was born in England and experienced on the stage. Betty, his wife, was an experienced radio actress specializing in juvenile parts, and took an unbilled role in a couple of the *Fu Manchu* broadcasts. When not excelling as Petrie, White headed his own successful radio-producing company. White was also in his third year as a regular on the *Adventures of Rin-Tin-Tin* radio program.

Back in the days when he was playing in *Three Wise Fools*, White married a girl in the cast, Betty Reynolds. She joined him in his radio ventures, and has been his partner ever since. Betty Reynolds played a supporting role in one episode of *The Shadow of Fu Manchu*.

Part way through the series, John C. Daly, (not, by the way, the John Charles Daly of television's *What's My Line* fame) was replaced by actor Harold Huber, and Sunda Love was replaced by a new character, played by Charles Manson. In the thirties, Huber became a popular character player for Warner Brothers, as well as a radio actor. He is also known to Charlie Chan fans for playing police inspectors of various nationalities in the 20th Century-Fox film series. Huber also wrote radio scripts for *Suspense* in 1943 and 1944.

Radio actress Sunda Love (mistakenly listed as Sundra Love) as the nefarious Fu Manchu.

During the first few weeks of the series, beautiful Sunda Love played the recurring role of Karamaneh, the exotic slave girl heroine who was secretly among Dr. Fu Manchu's agents. In those early adventures, Fu Manchu had no daughter. Karamaneh (whose name meant "slave" in her native Arabic) fell in love with Dr. Petrie and his feelings were mutual – though never confessed on the radio program, only suggested. Throughout the adventures, Karamaneh was loyal to her Chinese master, but stealthily schemed to keep Dr. Petrie and Nayland Smith from being killed in each of the devil doctor's maniacal death traps. It was also revealed that Karamaneh had a brother, one of Fu Manchu's slaves, and Fu held his life hostage against Karamaneh's obedience. By the end of December, her role was written out of the program after Dr. Petrie provided minor aid to liberate her brother, and she was free to flee from the evil Oriental.

Sunda Love was an exotic tall brunette who dates the start of her professional career back to the tender age of four, when she sang ballads in her father's motion picture house. At the age of five she saw her first stage show, *Pickled Peppers,* and determined, then and there, to become an actress. She was schooled in the William Owen Shakespearean Company, the University of Illinois, Northwestern, and the University of California. Stock company, club work and local broadcasts prepared her for stardom in *Tales of the Foreign Legion.*

Others in the cast included Robert Fiske, Peggy Davis, John Stamford and Isabel Randolph.

LEGAL COMPLICATIONS

When the McCann-Erickson Company, the ad agency representing the sponsor, Campana, secured permission from CBS to produce a weekly radio program based on the Fu Manchu novels in the spring of 1932, they ran into a temporary complication that almost prevented them from going into production.

For at least two months in the summer of 1932, there was a dispute regarding the radio rights to the Fu Manchu property. Nate Caldwell, head of a program checking bureau in Chicago, claimed he held an option with Rohmer for the American ether version and that under no circumstances could the serial be introduced on the air unless the adaptations prepared by him were used. Caldwell had at one time secured a contract with Sax Rohmer and went to the trouble of writing radio scripts for a proposed radio program that never met fruition. In negotiating the time with CBS, the Campana Company, at that time developing a radio serial based on Fu Manchu, was under the impression that the network had the exclusive rights to the scripts, and that the account would be free to select its own continuity writer.

The radio rights to the Sax Rohmer stories were controlled by Nate Caldwell since 1926, and for a time in 1928 it was on the air over KOIL in Omaha, Nebraska. That incarnation was an adaptation of *The Insidious Dr. Fu Manchu,* and if the newspapers from

Lincoln, Nebraska are correct, the name of the radio program was the same title. The program was a sustainer (no sponsor) and at the time the author waived royalties. Had the program gained a sponsor, Rohmer would have received royalties. The cast consisted of The Brandies Players, the station's repertory group.

By interpretation of a clause in the contract, Nate Caldwell maintained the option on the radio rights to Rohmer's mystery beyond the KOIL broadcasts, and it was Caldwell who convinced Fred Ibbett that Fu Manchu was a natural; the radio director readily agreed. Ibbett in turn convinced the Campana Company to sponsor the dramas through the McCann-Erickson advertising agency. Only after the deal was signed did Ibbett and the ad agency discover the stratagem: Caldwell's rejoinder was that CBS was merely acting as his agent in peddling the story to the cosmetic-maker and denied that, while granting the authority, he signed away any of his control.

The radio rights were indeed controlled by Nate Caldwell, and executives at McCann-Erickson were fully aware that instant popularity was ensured thanks to the public's familiarity with the character. *Fu Manchu*, the satanic Chinese mandarin, a best-seller for 15 years, had been three times dramatized on stage and six times photographed for the screen before arriving as a radio attraction after a period of negotiation. The three Paramount Pictures were tremendous hits for the studio and the upcoming Boris Karloff vehicle being filmed at MGM, which radio executives figured to piggyback on cross-promotion in regional areas, would be released in theaters circa October 1932. This, along with the contractual obligation for the time slot on CBS, put executives at McCann-Erickson into a bind.

A representative for the ad agency tried to get Caldwell to waive his rights for a flat consideration, but later maintained that he stay on as the continuity writer for the entire series… or he would create a legal scenario that could prevent the sponsor and ad agency from broadcasting the series. The contract with CBS and Campana Italian Balm was for a 52-week run starting September 28. Since the half-hour periods were scheduled dramatizations of Sax Rohmer's Dr. Fu Manchu series, behind-the-scenes discussions created a potential solution: if by mid-August the tangle over who controlled the rights to the Chinese melodrama was not straightened out, the sponsor would drop the idea entirely and instead move over *The First Nighter Program*, which they presently sponsored on NBC, to CBS. The contract with NBC was subject to a 30-days' notice prior to the expiration of the current 13-week lap, and notice to NBC to cancel the program would result in shifting the drama to CBS.

The First Nighter Program was at that time enjoying a healthy run of a second season, an anthology program meant to lure radio listeners to the make-believe world of the theater. From tragedy to romance, every episode was originally conceived with the theater-goer seeking a drama worthy of paying a general admission ticket. The intention was to capture the listening audience who relished a taste of blood and thunder with *Fu Manchu*, a different audience who listened to *The First Nighter Program* for a weekly dose of romance and comedy. After the dispute was straightened out with Caldwell, the ad agency formally requested the script writers of *First Nighter* to avoid any dramas of detective or mystery while the *Fu Manchu* program aired on another network. Caldwell, however, submitted the same 16 half-hour radio scripts dramatized over KOIL; then, beginning with broadcast No. 17, a serialized adaptation of the second novel, *The Return of Dr. Fu Manchu*, was dramatized on the program.

Before the premiere, Metro-Goldwyn-Mayer asked and received assurances of "protection" for its forthcoming *Mask of Fu Manchu* from Nate Porter Caldwell, who controlled the radio rights to all of Sax Rohmer's works. The radio program was to premiere two weeks prior to the release of the Metro picture. Metro wanted to be assured that the story featured in the movie would not be adapted for radio. Rohmer, meanwhile, was paid $150 per episode for the *Fu Manchu* radio serial.

The radio program dramatizes the malevolent doctor attempting to carry out his fiendish plan and further the cause of his political order from the Mandarin province of Ho-Nan. Fu Manchu summons a poisonous cat, fiery hands of death and a mummy to hunt down the Reverend Eltham and obtain the coveted name of a secret agent in China. Nayland Smith and Dr. Petrie are subjected to the tortures of the Wire Jacket and the Six Gates of Joyful Wisdom as they attempt to thwart the evil Doctor and they narrowly escape death on the moors of West England. A league of assassins, secret societies, and dens filled with opium addicts provided weekly pulp thrills.

In January 1933, three months after the premiere of *The Insidious Dr. Fu Manchu* and about the time the second serial began, Campana's Italian Balm concentrated all its advertising on radio, dropping all newsprint and supplementary forms for one week, which was designated as "National Campana week." The big radio push was for the purpose of moving the 10-cent size packages from the counters of Woolworth, Kresge, Grant and other emporiums. It was in a sense the acid test given to radio advertising's direct results on a large scale. Charles Hughes on *First Nighter*, and Bob White on *Fu Manchu*, took to the microphones to deliver special pleading with the public. They frankly put it up to the peasantry: "If you like these programs, help us prove that radio advertising pays, or these programs may be forced off the air, and you will be deprived of the pleasure they give you."

The First Nighter program received an overwhelming response, according to an inter-office memo at McCann-Erickson, while the *Fu Manchu* program received a response below expectations. By Valentine's, with the total tabulated, it was decided to scale back on advertising costs and CBS was notified that sponsorship for *Fu Manchu* would be dropped before the end of April. After all, the *Fu Manchu* program cost more to produce than *First Nighter*, especially since Nate Caldwell was receiving more money than the director for his involvement. The network maintained an option to pay Caldwell and Ibbett to continue production on the *Fu Manchu* program, in the hopes of luring a new sponsor to replace Campana, but the network rejected the option from Caldwell and ceased production after the broadcast of April 24.

COMPETITION

Beginning with the broadcast of December 2, 1932, the producers of *Five Star Theater* decided to replace their weekly offering of comedy (starring the Marx Brothers in a series of mis-adventures known as "Flywheel, Shyster and Flywheel") with weekly serialized adaptations of Earl Derr Biggers' Charlie Chan mysteries, starting with *The Black Camel*. Sponsored by the Standard Oil Company, executives at the McCann-Erickson advertising agency were hired to create a weekly program that would replicate the success of Ed Wynn's "Fire Chief" program. The weekly cost of production, however, was more expensive than most programs. By comparison, Ed Wynn's weekly salary was $1,500 less than what Groucho Marx was being paid. At the suggestion of an executive at McCann-Erickson, and observing the success of *The Insidious Dr. Fu Manchu*, the format of *Five Star Theater* was revised; The Marx Brothers were dropped in lieu of a mystery program dramatized in weekly installments. Enter stage left, adaptations of the Charlie Chan novels.

During the economic hardships of the Great Depression, pulps provided affordable content to the masses, and were one of the primary forms of entertainment, along with film and radio. Fran Striker, co-creator of *The Lone Ranger* and *The Green Hornet* radio programs, was a fan of pulp fiction, along with motion-pictures and adventure stories. The Fu Manchu novels undoubtedly inspired Striker to create his own rendition, a radio crime thriller titled *Warner Lester, Manhunter*, which premiered in the spring of 1932. In an effort to combat the popular *Eno Crime Club* mystery program, Striker was asked by James Jewell at radio station WXYZ in Detroit, Michigan to create and script a radio program that would replicate yarns commonplace in pulp magazines.

The title character was an independent private investigator who often profited from his adventures by stealing the money of murderers and blackmailers. As the announcer revealed in episode eight: "Lester is neither with the law, or definitely against the law. He occupies a rather peculiar position, on a line that is neither within nor yet without the law. His clever manner of thinking usually brings him the solution of a crime before the police are able to solve it, and he often profits thereby."

The series was so popular a spin-off series was created, titled *Manhunters*, featuring various crime dramas with rotating detective characters such as Peter Thorne of Scotland Yard. The mysteries would occasionally lean toward horror and science fiction with such plots as a mad movie producer using an octopus in a fiendish murder plan, another involving vengeful ghosts and another featuring a curse from ancient kings after scientists uncover an Egyptian tomb.

Perhaps the most challenging culprits for Warner Lester and his friend Mike Axford was The Crimson Fang Cult, led by Dr. Fang and his equally vile daughter. Obviously inspired by the Dr. Fu Manchu series in print and on screen, the crafty oriental used a variety of gimmicks such as a death ray in an attempt to assassinate the secretary of war. The criminal mastermind was so popular Striker was requested to write a short run radio program, a spin-off centering on Dr. Fang and his criminal exploits, lasting a total of 59 episodes titled *The Crimson Fang*. (At one time also titled *Manhunters-O-Fangs*.)

ORANGE BLOSSOMS

On the evening of March 1, 1937, Bransby Williams, stage actor, gave three varied and representative pieces from his repertoire over the BBC: "Orange Blossoms," a story of the East by Sax Rohmer, in which Bransby Williams gave a notable character study; his own monologue, "Old '94' On Time," which he broadcast in August last year and in which he gives a whimsical sketch of an old man giving his opinion on time; and finally, "The Charge of the Light Brigade" by Tennyson. "Orange Blossoms" was a musical monologue written for a music hall by Rohmer in 1921, one of more than half a dozen he wrote in his lifetime.

RADIO LUXEMBOURG

During the thirties, the pirate commercial radio programs transmitted from the European continent had vast English audiences. By law, the British Broadcasting Corporation had a complete monopoly on radio transmission within Britain, and was charged by its license holders, and by the British Parliament, with the task of providing radio entertainment for all tastes. Commercial radio, banned in Britain and able to operate only from transmitters on the Continent, capitalized on this situation. With the financial backing of sponsors such as Ponds, Colgate-Palmolive, and other large firms, the pirate stations attracted quality writers and performers to provide showcases for their talents, which the BBC could not match. From the inception of their transmissions until they were closed down in the late thirties, the pirate IBC stations in Luxembourg, Normandy, Lyons and Toulouse offered a continuous flow of high-quality entertainment. In 1936, Radio Luxembourg decided to feature a series of mystery adventures built around a single character. This series would originally be written and supervised by Sax Rohmer himself.

"Sax himself wrote the scripts during the first half of the series," Cay Van Ash, Rohmer's assistant and biographer later recalled. "When the series continued beyond his original expectations, he found it too great an imposition on his time. He continued to write some of the scripts, but others were written either by Elizabeth or myself. I came in on only the last six months or so of the project. I had first met Sax in November 1935, and he had had my education in hand for just over a year. Whether the draft scripts were written by Elizabeth or by me, they were carefully edited afterwards by Sax, for which reason I described the series in Master of Villainy as the most faithful version broadcast. The adaptation was not a very difficult job. I don't recall that any particular selection of episodes was made. As I remember it, we just went straight through the books in their natural sequence. The dialogue did not require changing very much. On the other hand, we did our utmost to avoid narration and to translate action directly into dialogue or sound. This often required additional material, and I think we also used a great many more sound effects than there were in the American *Shadow of Fu Manchu* radio series."

The November 1936 issue of *Radio Pictorial* featured the following news blurb: "Still running the rule over some of the December entertainments from the Continent, we come to the adventures of Sax Rohmer's Fu Manchu. By December 27th the program, which starts Sunday the 6th, will no doubt have become favorite with listeners, and so after the Christmas festivals you can be thrilled in no small measure."

Frank Cochrane, who played the Luxembourg-broadcast Fu Manchu, was a distinguished stage actor and eminently suited to play the part of Dr. Fu Manchu. He had lived for many years in China, studying the native habits and mental makeup. He had also played innumerable Chinese roles on the stage. (Cochrane had won acclaim for the part of The Cobbler in the long-running show, *Chu-Chin-Chow*.)

"Fu Manchu," Cochrane said in a 1937 interview, "has a definite personality and a definite purpose. He is a keen wit and possesses a quick Oriental brain. He is a demon for power and wants to mold the world to his way of direction and thinking. The adventures of Dr. Fu Manchu are full of unlikely happenings, which have been so well treated that they convince the listener as being highly probable. Before settling down to listen, I suggest you turn out the lights in the room the moment you hear the gong and take your mind into serious channels. This will help you enormously to catch the illusion."

All of the IBC recordings were produced in London. There were no live broadcasts. It is believed that Rohmer and the crew recorded the shows at a disused theater. The leading light in the operation was producer Eddie Pola, who also took part as an actor in some episodes. There was actually a plan to follow up the 52 Fu Manchu broadcasts with a series adapted from Rohmer's *The Quest of the Sacred Slipper* (1919), Cay Van Ash distinctly remembering having written the first two episodes. However, the BBC exerted legal pressure to close down the rival operation, so it came to nothing.

D.A. Clarke-Smith, a well-known stage actor who had appeared in Rohmer's stage plays *The Eyes of Siva* and *Secret Egypt*, played the role of Nayland Smith. "I'm getting hardened to it now, but the nerve strain is still almost unbelievable," commented Clarke-Smith, as the atmosphere in the studio grew more intense with each passing moment. "I have to talk so fast, six or seven prop men are grouped round another mike, to provide the dramatic effects. And, when I'm supposed to be swimming for my life in a swirling river, I have to try to forget that at the other mike a man is vigorously shaking a half-filled hot-water bottle."

The program's producer, swift-thinking Eddie Pola, rehearsed three radio installments in the space of two hours. "Funniest thing, rehearsing one dramatic scene," recalled Eddie, "was when we came to the line, 'Shoot the man at the window.' The effects man fired the gun, but it just didn't go off. Again we repeated, 'Shoot the man at the window.' Again the gun refused to function. We tried again. 'Shoot the man at the window!' But still the gun was silent. 'Oh, cut his throat,' I said. And at that moment, the gun went off and nearly blew me out of my skin!"

"There is only one female role in *Dr. Fu Manchu*," Frank Cochrane said. "This is the part of the heroine. The girl who takes this character, Karamaneh, is Rani Walker. She's brilliant! There is a good cast in these programs, all exceptionally good actors, and with Rani in the only female role – who, as I have said, is excellent. It is a well-balanced cast."

The supporting cast who performed the incidental character parts included Arthur Young, Mervyn Johns (father of actress Glynis Johns), and Vernon Kelso. As was common in radio drama, the actors often took several parts in the same episode and program, and sometimes switched roles whenever necessary. For example, in Episode 43, Arthur Young portrayed Dr. Fu Manchu, Inspector Weymouth, and Sir Frank Narcombe, while Vernon Kelso took on three other parts.

With the completion of the Fu Manchu series, Cochrane and Clarke-Smith were rated such a successful team that they were featured in another long-running series of radio plays, this time concerning Inspector Brooks of Scotland Yard. Clarke-Smith played the Inspector, while Cochrane played the – perhaps inevitably – Chinese villain, La Sante.

W.O.G. Lofts and R.E. Briney did some excellent research on this pirate radio station, and especially the *Fu Manchu* radio rendition, for their article "Sh-h-h! Dr. Fu Manchu is on the Air." According to their article, the Radio Luxembourg rendition consisted of fifty-two 15-minute episodes, broadcast every Sunday at 7 p.m. from December 6, 1936 to November 28, 1937. Following the completion of the series, episodes #19 through #28 were repeated, lasting from December 5, 1937 until February 6, 1938, when transmission ended. Earlier, the first eleven episodes had been repeated in a different time-slot: Wednesdays at 4:45 p.m., from July 21 through September 29, 1937. The entire series of fifty-two episodes was also broadcast over Radio Lyons, Sundays at 10:15 P.M., from March 7, 1937 to March 6, 1938. Thus, for an eleven week period during the summer of 1937, listeners to the pirate radio stations could hear Dr. Fu Manchu three times a week---three different episodes, at three different times.

In a letter to R. E. Briney, dated May 1, 1973, Cay Van Ash noted that Sax Rohmer wrote the scripts during the first half of the series. Thereafter, when the series continued beyond his original expectations, he found it too great an imposition on his time. He continued to write some of the scripts, but others were written either by Elizabeth or Cay Van Ash. In *Master of Villainy,* Cay Van Ash referred to those fifty-two episodes as "the most faithful versions of the original stories that have so far appeared 'on the air.'"

CAST:

Fu Manchu: Frank Cochrane
Nayland Smith: D. A. Clarke-Smith
Dr. Petrie: Jack Lambert (1-9), John Rae (10-24), Gordon
   McLeod (27-43) and Cameron Hall (44-52)
Karamaneh: Pamela Titheradge and later Rani Waller

Other actors included Arthur Young, Mervyn Johns and Vernon Kelso.

Episode #1, "The Painted Kiss" (December 6, 1936)
Episode #2, "The Clue of the Pigtail" (December 13, 1936)
Episode #3, "The Mystery of the Red Moat" (December 20, 1936)
Episode #4, "The Green Mist" (December 27, 1936)
Episode #5, "The Call of Siva" (January 3, 1937)
Episode #6, "The Hulk of the Flats" (January 10, 1937)
Episode #7, "The Brain Thief" (January 17, 1937)
Episode #8, "Aaron's Rod" (January 24, 1937)
Episode #9, "The Living Dead" (January 31, 1937)
Episode #10, "The Fungi Cellars" (February 7, 1937)
Episode #11, "The Lord of Fires" (February 14, 1937)
Episode #12, "The Wire Jacket" (February 21, 1937)
Episode #13, "The Cry of the Nighthawk" (February 28, 1937)
Episode #14, "The White Peacock" (March 7, 1937)
Episode #15, "The Coughing Horror" (March 14, 1937)
Episode #16, "The Capture of Karamaneh" (March 21, 1937)
Episode #17, "The Silver Buddha" (March 28, 1937)
Episode #18, "The Terror Tower" (April 4, 1937)
Episode #19, "The Fiery Hand" (April 11, 1937)
Episode #20, "The Return of Aziz" (April 18, 1937)
Episode #21, "The Six Gates" (April 25, 1937)
Episode #22, "The Mummy" (May 2, 1937)
Episode #23, "The Brass Box" (May 9, 1937)
Episode #24, "The Flower of Silence" (May 16, 1937)
Episode #25, "The Golden Pomegranates" (May 23, 1937)
Episode #26, "The Adventure of the Queen of Hearts" (May 30, 1937)
Episode #27, "The Xagazig Mystery" (June 6, 1937)
Episode #28, "The House of Hashish" (June 13, 1937)
Episode #29, "The Lillies of Death" (June 20, 1937)
Episode #30, "Lady of the Si-Fan" (June 27, 1937)
Episode #31, "The House of the Wild Cat" (July 4, 1937)
Episode #32, "The Lion Crypt" (July 11, 1937)

Episode #33, "The Flying Death" (July 18, 1937)
Episode #34, "The Shadow Army" (July 25, 1937)
Episode #35, "Satan's Chapel" (August 1, 1937)
Episode #36, "The Purple Shadow" (August 8, 1937)
Episode #37, "The Flying Plague" (August 15, 1937)
Episode #38, "The House of the Devil Doctor" (August 22, 1937)
Episode #39, "The Hairless Horror" (August 29, 1937)
Episode #40, "The Scented Drug" (September 5, 1937)
Episode #41, "The Devil Doctor's Daughter" (September 12, 1937)
Episode #42, "The Flower of Eternal Life" (September 19, 1937)
Episode #43, "The Return of the Monk" (September 26, 1937)
Episode #44, "The Big Raid" (October 3, 1937)
Episode #45, "The Arrest of the Devil Doctor" (October 10, 1937)
Episode #46, "The Secret of the Living Dead" (October 17, 1937)
Episode #47, "The Sleeping Venus" (October 24, 1937)
Episode #48, "The Vault of the Living Dead" (October 31, 1937)
Episode #49, "The House of the Bloodhound" (November 7, 1937)
Episode #50, "Man Made Gold" (November 14, 1937)
Episode #51, "The Human Incinerator" (November 21, 1937)
Episode #52, "The Hell Below the Thames" (November 28, 1937)

Oddly, *Variety* reported more than 52 episodes. "After a run of over a year, episode No. 62 brings the Dr. Fu Manchu broadcasts from Luxembourg to an end on February 6. So successful have these thrillers been, J. Walter Thompson, on behalf of the manufacturers of [Phillips Dental Magnesia] is replacing them with a new series of *Inspector Brookes of Scotland Yard*. Each mystery will take three Sundays to unravel. First episode is 'The Poison Handkerchief Murder.' Dr. Fu Manchu will continue from Radio Lyons until March 6. Inspector Brookes commencing from this station on the following Sunday." If the radio programs continued once a week from the November 28, 1937 broadcast, the 62nd episode would certainly have been aired on February 6, 1938, as *Variety* indicated. Further digging revealed Lofts and Briney were indeed correct: episodes 19 through 28 were repeated through February 6, 1938.

WHAT HAPPENED AT 8:20?

Similar to the American rendition of *The Adventures of Ellery Queen,* this bi-weekly mystery anthology provided leading authors of mystery fiction an opportunity to script an original story with solution. Multiple guest panelists would listen to the brief radio drama, lasting an average of 12 to 14 minutes, then be provided four to five minutes to review the clues and solve the mystery. During this downtime, musical entertainment was provided to the radio audience. After which, the program would conclude with the panelists given an opportunity to solve the crime. Every episode began at 8:00 p.m. and concluded at 8:30. Twenty minutes into the broadcast, a crime was committed (hence the title of the program) and each story took place in a location where music would become the centerpiece of the drama. The program was created by James Langham. Under the production of Ronald Waldman and Herbert Browne, the series lasted a mere six broadcasts. They were recorded and later aired in Australia in the fall of 1939. The following are summaries of each broadcast.

Episode #1, "The Strange Affair at the Old Dutch Mill" (October 7, 1938)

Music was provided by the Flying Dutchmen Dance Band and the BBC Revue Chorus.

Scripted by John Rhode, author of *The Motor Rally Mystery.*

Cast: Clifford Bean (the waiter), Maurice Denham (Inspector Waghorn), Bryan Herbert (Mr. Van Lune), Barbara MacFadycan (Kitty), Robert Marshall (Mr. Silver), Reginald Purdell (Clarence Condotti), Bryan Powley (Conrad), and Norman Shelley (Superintendent Hanslet).

Plot: In the old Dutch Mill, a cheerful road house with orchestra and entertainment, a number of people are gathered together for the evening. When a brutal murder occurs, Superintendent Hanslet performs his detective skills to solve the crime based on the characters and clues he observed earlier in the evening.

Episode #2, "The Mystery of the Grand Duke's Emerald" (October 21, 1938)
Music was provided by Ivor Dennis at the piano.
Scripted by Anthony Armstrong, author of *The Ten Minute Alibi*.
Cast: Bruce Carfax (Ray Ramon), Bebe Daniels (Emerald Avonside), Francis de Wolff (Captain Maxwell), Vernon Harris (Mr. Marble), Howard Marion-Crawford (Gus Finckel), Murray Moncrieff (Monsieur Pierre), Mary O'Farrell (The Honorable Mrs. Bates), and Willeen Wilson (Betty Amor).
Plot: The theft of an Emerald takes place during a private party at a London restaurant.

Episode #3, "The Curious Affair at the Ship's Concert" (November 4, 1938)
Music provided by Phil Cardew and his Band.
Scripted by Arnold Ridley, author of *The Ghost Train*.
Cast: Clifford Bean (the steward), Clephan Bell (the doctor), Patricia Burke (Gloria Gordon), Maurice Denham (the officer *and* Ted), Peter Ducrow (Dunce), Eileen Erskine (Anne Conway), Robert Graham (Jack Stoner), Howard Marion-Crawford (Simmonds), David Miller (Barney), Mary O'Farrell (Miss Cooper-Bardie), Norman Shelley (Captain McGuire), and Richard Wattis (Tony Twining).
Plot: A luxury liner at sea rolling home from Rio, a fog blowing up, and a ship's concert about to get under away set the stage. The ingredients include a jazz band leader, a petty crooner, a rich old woman and a cryptic radio message saying "Satisfied No Crooks Aboard."

Episode #4, "The Mysterious Voice in St. George's Hall" (November 18, 1938)

Music provided by the BBC Variety Orchestra, conducted by Charles Shadwell.

Script by Eric Maschwitz, author of *Death at Broadcasting House*.

Cast: Ronald Frankau (*unknown*), Greta Gynt (the actress), Rudy Starita (*unknown*) and Hal Yates (the man with the American accent).

Plot: A famous actress is broadcasting in St. George's Music Hall, headquarters of BBC Variety, when something happens at 8:20. The cast of characters include the radio crew: the producer, the producer's assistant, the sound effects operator, the chief producer, and a studio attendant.

Episode #5, "The Strange Story of a Dance Record" (December 2, 1938)

Music provided by Phil Cardew and his Band.

Script and music composed by Spike Hughes.

Cast: Oliver Burt (Jake), Maurice Denham (a policeman), Ronnie Hill (Billy), Janet Lind (Kay Waring), Douglas Matthews (Dr. Scott), Bryan Powley (recording manager Morris), Bill Quest (Irving), and Richard Wattis (band leader Al).

Plot: The scene of the crime occurs at a recording studio in London.

Episode #6, "The Peculiar Case at the Poppy Club" (December 16, 1938)

Music provided by Phil Cardew and his Band.

Script and songs composed by Sax Rohmer.

Cast: Clifford Bean (Chang), Patricia Burke (Suzee), D.A. Clarke-Smith (Nayland Smith), Gilbert Davis (Dr. Petrie), Ike Hatch (Sambo), Hamilton Price (Inspector Woodford), and Jack Train (Sergeant Hull).

Plot: The Poppy Club is a little place in Limehouse, and it was to that quarter of London that Nayland Smith, special investigator for Scotland Yard, gets out one winter's evening. His intention was to arrest a notorious character known as Rio Shang, a remorseless killer employed by the master criminal, Dr. Fu Manchu. Now, unfortunately, Nayland Smith was unacquainted with the appearance of this man, Rio Chang, but he had reason to believe that Chang was in London. And so, on the night of the peculiar case at the Poppy Club, we find Nayland Smith, accompanied by his friend, Dr. Petrie, arriving at Limehouse Police Station, and interviewing Divisional-Inspector Woodford.

"The Peculiar Case at the Poppy Club" was an original story written for radio. Rohmer later rewrote it as a short story called "Supper at the Poppy Club" in 1941. A.P. Watt & Company, Rohmer's British literary agents, attempted to place the story in various magazines or newspapers in 1941 and 1942, but were unsuccessful. China was an ally during the war and this was one of several setbacks for Rohmer's most lucrative property at the time.

MYSELF AND GASTON MAX

Among Sax Rohmer's fictional detectives was Major Bernard de Treville, known to his friends as "Trevvy," who was considered a magnet for crime. Assisted by his friend, "Digger," who also recounts the adventures *a la* Dr. Watson, the Major solves many an improbable case involving master criminals and international intrigue. At least 16 short stories were published in the pages of *This Week* magazine, from 1937 to 1945, and six of them were adapted for a brief series over BBC Radio.

> Episode #1, "The Black and White Bag" by Sax Rohmer (August 21, 1942)
> Episode #2, "The Kravonia Panelling" (August 28, 1942)
> Episode #3, "The Green Turban" (September 4, 1942)
> Episode #4, "White Jackdaws are Rare" (September 11, 1942)
> Episode #5, "Count d'Ambro's Window" (September 18, 1942)
> Episode #6, "The Broken Eagle" (September 25, 1942)

The above information contradicts the exact order of broadcast dates and script titles reported in *The Rohmer Review* (No. 15, September 1976). The information contained in this book originates from archival materials and should be accurate versus what was reported in *The Rohmer Review*.

For the radio incarnation, the lead character from the printed page was replaced with M. Gaston Max, Rohmer's French detective who appeared in three novels prior to the radio incarnation. Sax Rohmer, Elizabeth Rohmer and Cay Van Ash each wrote two radio scripts, with Rohmer supervising and revising the scripts before rehearsals. The dates of publication from which the radio scripts were adapted are listed for reference:

"The Black and White Bag" (*This Week*, September 12, 1937)
"The Broken Ikon" (*This Week*, September 19, 1937)
"Count d'Ambro's Window" (*This Week*, January 9, 1938)
"The Mystery of the Panelled Room" (*This Week*, July 30, 1939)
"The Mystic Turban" (*This Week*, August 13, 1939)
"The Elusive Jackdaw" (*This Week*, August 20, 1939)

Carleton Hobbs as Gaston Max
James Woodburn as Angus Macgregor
Produced by John Richmond.
6:35 p.m. to 7 pm.

M. Gaston Max, of the Paris police, was the pivital hero in a series of four detective novels, the first of which served as a Fu Manchu prototype – the mysterious Mr. King, a deal in drugs and head of a Yellow Peril organization known throughout underworld circles as "The Sublime Order." Titled *The Yellow Claw* (1915). At the time the novel was written, such menace was only dominant in adventure fiction. Renditions of both comic strip and silver screen would not become common until the 1930s with such portrayals of Fu Manchu, Ming the Merciless on *Flash Gordon*, and The Dragon Lady in *Terry and the Pirates*. But Rohmer discovered the formula offered opportunity to establish a variation-on-a-theme through further adventures.

In his sequel, *The Golden Scorpion* (1920), Rohmer established M. Gaston Max as a master of disguise. When another criminal organization threatens the whole of London, Detective Inspector Dunbar investigates. Initially he expected help from Max, as he had in the first novel, but the body of the famous detective was found by the River Police. Only later in the novel is it discovered that the unnamed cabbie, at the center of events, is Gaston Max in disguise. The antagonist of this novel was revealed to be an agent of Dr. Fu Manchu, who appears in person but is never referenced by name. This established the four M. Gaston Max detective novels to take place in the same literary universe as the Fu Manchu novels.

The third novel, *The Day the World Ended* (1930), incorporated an old dark house feel suggesting the work of blood-sucking vampires and a strange man dressed in armor roaming the castle hall. Once again, M. Gaston Max appears late in the novel, having been in disguise for much of the adventure. The solution is revealed as the work of a strange scientist who is attempting to use his scientific achievements (including a death ray) to conquer the world.

The fourth and final novel, *Seven Sins* (1944), was based on an eight-part serial in *Collier's* magazine (as were the other three novels), with M. Gaston Max assisting with the war cause. A British lord finds a dead body on the couch in his living room and notifies the police. An investigation is launched by Scotland Yard, with Max answering the call to help track down a Nazi spy. It seems the murder ties in with Max's present investigation involving a gambling ring, an Egyptian mummy and dozens of suspects. The Nazis are eventually unmasked at the end of the adventure.

Because the M. Gaston Max mysteries were part of the Fu Manchu universe, it seemed fitting to include information regarding the 1942 radio serial in this book.

THE NIGHTINGALE

Having worked professionally as a song writer and comedy sketch writer for music hall performers before settling down to a career writing fiction, Rohmer never turned down an offer to revisit his past. Rohmer co-wrote the book and lyrics with Michael Martin-Harvey for a new Lee Ephraim musical, *The Nightingale*, broadcast over the BBC on the evening of August 15, 1947. Produced by Jack Hulbert, the broadcast originated from the Princess's Theatre in London, England.

THE SHADOW OF FU MANCHU

Campana maintained an option for renewal with Sax Rohmer until August of 1933, but having decided to stick with *The First Nighter* program and not renew *Fu Manchu* meant Rohmer could explore other options. Multiple offers were heavily weighed and Rohmer ultimately chose to sign a contract with Radio Attractions, located in the RKO Building in New York City. Offers from radio producers varied but the lure for signing with Radio Attractions was syndication – the practice of leasing transcription discs to radio stations across the country (and internationally) for regional coverage with local sponsorship to exceed coverage offered through a broadcast network.

In April of 1938, Sax Rohmer arrived in New York City, from London, for a one-week business trip and to sign contracts with Radio Attractions, and with Republic Pictures – the latter of whom wanted to produce a cliffhanger serial based on Sax Rohmer's character. This would ultimately lead to the creation of *The Drums of Fu Manchu*, initially proposed at Republic as *The Return of Fu Manchu*. (Columbia Pictures was in negotiations to produce a cliffhanger serial based on Sax Rohmer's character, but Republic won out.) Having signed with both parties, Rohmer's creation would ultimately become the hot topic of a new radio program and a filmed serial. *The Drums of Fu Manchu* would ultimately be adapted into this new radio production.

Bob Thompson wrote the scripts, adapted from Rohmer's novels; and from the story treatment for the newly conceived *The Drums of Fu Manchu*. Publicity sent out to magazines and newspapers claimed Rohmer himself wrote the radio scripts, but this was inaccurate. The cast consisted of Hanley Stafford (Sir Nayland Smith),

Meet FU MANCHU

By Steve Turnbull

Gale Gordon (Dr. James Petrie), Theodore Osborne (Dr. Fu Manchu), Edmond O'Brien (Inspector Rhymer), and Paula Winslow (Kamarenth). Other members of the cast included Lee Millar, Jerry Mour, Frank Nelson, Norman Fields and Eric Snowden. Gerald Mohr has often been credited as the announcer in reference guides but

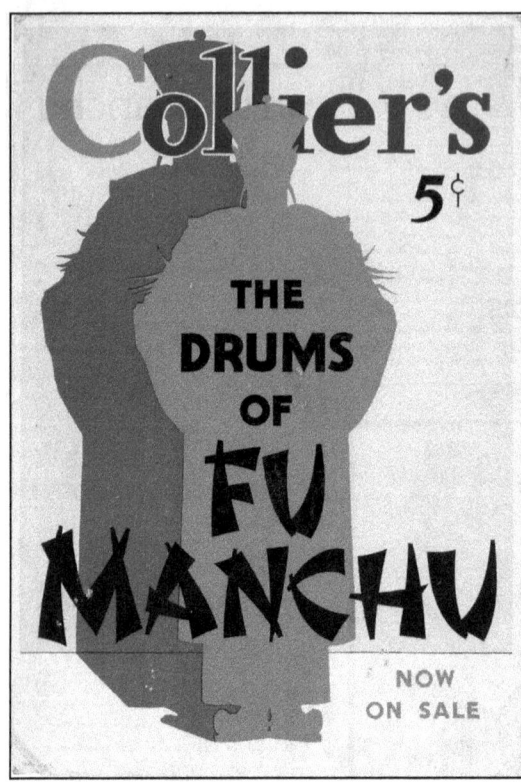

paperwork verifies Edmond O'Brien as the narrator.

The entire program was recorded in two batches, under the direction of Norman Wilson. Production was overseen by Jack Lewis, who was responsible for *Ports of Call*. The first batch of 78 episodes was recorded in October and November of 1938, produced by Fields Brothers Radio Corp., cut by Radio Recorders, Inc. In June of 1939, a second batch of 78 episodes was produced with the same cast – but with one exception. Lou Marcelle, KFWB Hollywood announcer-actor, was cast in the lead role of Dr. Fu Manchu, verified through production files.

The second batch was recorded at the newly-equipped offices at 6253 Hollywood Blvd., with a custom-built public address system, remote lines and playback machine. The equipment was built and installed by C.C. McDonald, Hollywood recording engineer, by early February 1939. The new quarters included, besides executive offices, an audition room, production division, and a complete music and transcription library department.

The second series of 78 transcribed episodes were distributed direct from its West Coast offices. The first series was distributed by Radio Attractions in New York. Disc labels vary among collectors, and this split distribution method is the reason for what resulted in confusion over the years regarding the name of the company responsible for producing the discs.

Radio Attractions, located in New York City, gave a pre-hearing of its first production, *The Shadow of Fu Manchu*, to a group of advertising agency radio executives, station representatives, station managers and the trade press at a cocktail party at the Waldorf-Astoria Hotel, on December 7, 1939. The first two episodes were played for the audience, who were also told of the company's plan for helping stations and sponsors purchasing the program series to popularize the program by supplying them with tie-in promotion. In addition

Full page advertisements in *Broadcasting* magazine from 1938 and 1939, promoting *The Shadow of Fu Manchu* discs to radio station managers.

to the usual window and display cards and tickets to "The Radioside Theatre," the company offered *Fu Manchu* masks and picture buttons, fortune-telling incense, a Chinese key trick and a special edition of the story, as well as mats for use in advertising the program.

Latrobe, Pennsylvania, known as the birthplace for Arnold Palmer and the banana split, was the center of attraction for *The Shadow of Fu Manchu*, in January of 1939, when a new production aired for the first time over KDKA. On the evening of January 18, a Chinese party was held at the radio station to celebrate the premiere of a new radio program. There was a slinky Fu Manchu creeping about the walls as an estimated 100 people ate a Chinese dinner served by Chinese girls in costume. The radio station arranged the bash, inviting advertising prospects, agency folks, local sponsors of other radio programs and their wives to the event. Chopsticks were souvenirs. Charley Urquhart, production chief, appeared as old Fu Manchu himself and he was in most perfect makeup. After the dinner, everyone attending went to another studio for the presentation of the first two recordings.

Another preview presentation of *The Shadow of Fu Manchu* was put on by WHEC in Rochester, New York, on February 28. The preview guests were also provided with a Chinese supper, shown the opening chapters of the serial, and escorted around WHEC's studios by Chief Announcer Ken French, dressed as Dr. Fu Manchu.

There was a fourth full dress preview held at station KANS in Wichita, Kansas, featuring the same dinner and costume dress. These dinners were the result of a policy from Radio Attractions. Radio stations purchasing the transcription series were required to put up the cash and commit themselves to buy the series regardless of whether they had a sponsor. The system was to guarantee Radio Attractions against the station taking a "well, we'll sell something else" attitude. This was the common experience of many transcription houses in the past years that turned over audition recordings to stations, but did not demand deposits. On many occasions stations would play a transcription as a weekend filler, without paying for the rights, then sending the discs back and insisting they were unable to attract a sponsor. The gala dinners were to attract advertisers.

It should be noted that the first two episodes that aired over radio stations, and played back for the guests of those three dinner parties, were the same discs sent to radio stations across the country labeled as "Audition #1" and "Audition #2," but were indeed the first two episodes of the series. (Many times producers create an audition record but the audition was never meant for broadcast.)

The initial plan by Radio Attractions was to release a new serial program every other month, with *The Shadow of Fu Manchu*, *Ella Cinders* and *Hopalong Cassidy* among the first three. The last two were never produced. It was announced in February 1939 by Harry David Fields, executive vice-president, production on *Hopalong Cassidy* would begin in March, along with continuation of the *Fu Manchu* series. The cowboy yarn never met fruition and the company instead produced *The Adventures of Pinocchio*. By November 1939, they were syndicating their second production, *The Adventures of Pinocchio*.

Beginning January 16, 1939, *The Shadow of Fu Manchu* aired over WRVA in Richmond, Virginia, broadcast three times a week, sponsored by Larus & Bro. Co., in the interest of Domino cigarettes. Beginning the first Monday in February, the program was heard over KHJ under the 20 Grand cigarette bankroll (The Axton-Fisher

---

Fu Manchu Comes to KRNT, WMT and KMA,

THE dramatic mystery series featuring The Shadow of Fu Manchu, founded on the stories written by Sax Rohmer, will open on KRNT, WMT and KMA at 10:15 p. m.

THE DRAMAS will be broadcast at 4:45 p. m. WMT Tuesdays, Thursdays and Saturdays for the younger audience. KRNT will be broadcasting on those days at 5:30 p. m. and KMA will be airing the thrillers at 5:45 p. m.

THE SERIES is sponsored in the interest of "the 5,000 carrier salesmen of the Register and Tribune."

For 25 years Collier's magazine has been featuring Fu Manchu stories regularly.

Tobacco Company), heard three times a week, Monday, Wednesday and Friday. The program was a success for the sponsor, who expanded sponsorship over KFRC in San Francisco in mid-March.

Beginning March 1939, the *Des Moines Register & Tribune* agreed to sponsor the program on four stations including KRNT in Des Moines, WMT in Cedar Rapids, KMA, Shenandoah, Iowa and WNAX in Yankton, South Dakota.

Beginning April, the Crown Drug Company sponsored the program over KCMO in Kansas City. Starting May 1, the program was heard over WOR in New York City, sponsored by the American Beverage Company, promoting Dr. Brown's Celery Tonic.

From June 26, 1939 to June 28, 1940, two different stations aired the program under the sponsorship of the Fred Tregaskes Company in Phoenix, Arizona, product U.S. Tires. Beginning in July of 1939, the program went under sponsorship of Eno Salts over KHJ, beginning with broadcast #79 in the series.

The radio program aired over 75 stations in Canada starting in the fall of 1939. (On some stations two episodes were aired back-to-back as a half hour feature versus a 15-minute daily presentation.)

The Shadow of Fu Manchu launched on the evening of October 9, WMC in Memphis, Tennessee, under the sponsorship of the D. & C. Chemical Company, pitching Di-Min-Glo Wax. The Keck Furniture Company sponsored the program over WROK in Rockford.

During the same months, some stations across the country aired the program sustaining, hoping to gain a sponsor such as WTMJ in Milwaukee, and KWK in St. Louis. Beginning October 30, 1939, the Swift Canadian Co. of Toronto, selling meat products, through the J. Walter Thompson Company in Chicago, began sponsoring the program three times a week on a group of Canadian stations.

Opening the new year on January 1, 1940, *The Columbus Dispatch* sponsored the program over WBNS in Columbus, Ohio, to promote its "carrier boy" routes.   Beginning February 4, 1940, the Noss Pretzel & Cone Company of Cleveland, Ohio sponsored the program on WHK in Cleveland, Sunday evenings from 5 to 5:30 p.m., with two episodes back to back to form a half-hour weekly program.

By March of 1940, the program was picked up by three additional stations: The Dodge Dealers Association, Baltimore, Maryland, WFBR; Spear & Company (department store), Pittsburgh, Pennsylvania, KDKA; and Canton Provision Company (Pioneer meats), Canton, Ohio, WHBC.

By May 15, 1940, recent sponsors included Buffalo Rock, soft drink distributors, on WAPI, Birmingham; Friedman Clothes on WEST in Easton, Pennsylvania; and Red & White Stores on KHQ, Spokane. Rock Island Beverage began sponsoring in Moline, Illinois, over WHBF, in August of 1941. *The Shadow of Fu Manchu* premiered in the mid-Hudson valley in December 1941, in Poughkeepsie New York.

The Royal Men's Clothiers Shop was sponsor over KGU in Hawaii beginning in April 1941. In October of the same year, WMAS in Springfield, Massachusetts, began airing the program with Warwicks, a credit clothiers, as sponsor.

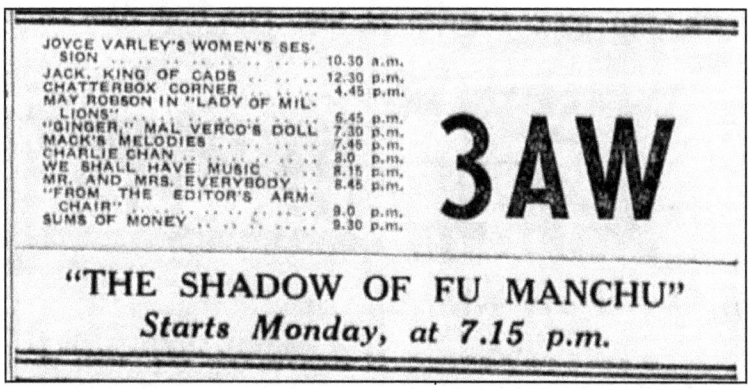

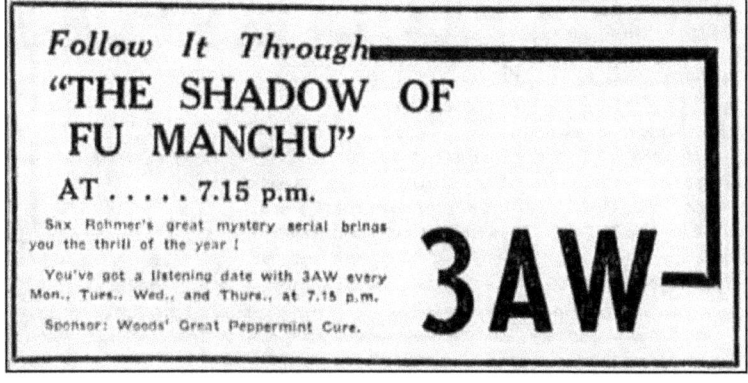

These, of course, are just a small list of the many radio stations across the country that aired *The Shadow of Fu Manchu* in the United States. The last known to be documented was in 1944 over a radio station in Cumberland, Maryland.

Overseas the program was heard in Australia beginning in April 1939. W.E. Woods, Ltd., Sydney, Australia (Wood's Great Peppermint Care), thru Gotham Asia Pty., Ltd.; that city, on April 10 starts sponsoring *Fu Manchu* on 2GB, Sydney; 3AW, Melbourne; 3SR, Victoria; 5DN, Adelaide and 5RM, Renmark on April 13; 3HA Western District on April 19; and 4BH, Brisbane on April 24; and 2GZ, New South Wales at the rate of four programs weekly. *Fu Manchu* was purchased in Australia and New Zealand by Macquarie Broadcasting Services. Sydney, W.E. Woods Ltd., has sponsored many important American transcriptions in recent years, including *The Count of Monte Carlo* and *Charlie Chan*.

The adaptations were quite faithful to the original books, though in the middle of the radio series the episodes occur out of sequential order by publication. From what is known so far:

Episodes #1 to #21, from *The Insidious Dr. Fu Manchu* (1913)
Episodes #22 to #27 from *The Hand of Fu Manchu* (1917)
Episodes #28 to #39 from *The Return of Dr. Fu Manchu* (1916)
Episodes #40 to #??? from *Trail of Fu Manchu* (1934)
Episodes #??? to #78 from *President of Fu Manchu* (1936)
Episodes #79 to #96 from *Daughter of Fu Manchu* (1931)
Episodes #97 to #117 from *Mask of Fu Manchu* (1932)
Episodes #118 to #137 from *Drums of Fu Manchu* (1939)
Episodes #138 to #156 from *Bride of Fu Manchu* (1933)

For decades the first 40 episodes were available in collector hands. Soon after an article documenting the history of Fu Manchu on radio appeared in *Scarlet Street* magazine, mentioning how additional discs were available for sale by a profiteering collector in Niles, Ohio; Ted Davenport of Radio Memories sought out the collector and purchased the discs. Since then many of the "lost" episodes were made available to collectors. To date, the entire run of

Disc label from Radio Attractions with episode number.
(Photo courtesy of Travis Conner.)

all 156 episodes are still not available in collector hands because a number of the discs are still lost.

The shows themselves had no script titles, just broadcast numbers, to assist stations in airing them in consecutive order. Throughout the 1980s, however, collectors of old-time radio created descriptive titles or plot summaries, often referred to as "collector titles," which carried over into mail order catalogs, fanzines and internet radio logs. The most commonly-accepted titles are those created by historian Ray Stanich, who reported the following episode titles and airdates in *The Rohmer Review*:

1. 05/08/39 The Insidious Dr. Fu-Manchu
2. 05/10/39 The Zayat Kiss
3. 05/12/39 The Zayat Kiss
4. 05/15/39 The Clue of the Pigtail
5. 05/17/39 The Clue of the Pigtail
6. 05/19/39 Red Moat
7. 05/22/39 Red Moat

8. 05/24/39 The Green Mist
9. 05/26/39 The Green Mist
10. 05/29/39 The Call of Siva
11. 05/31/39 The Call of Siva
12. 06/02/39 Karamaneh
13. 06/05/39 Karamaneh
14. 06/07/39 Andaman – Second!
15. 06/09/39 Andaman – Second!
16. 06/12/39 The Golden Flask
17. 06/14/39 The Golden Flask
18. 06/16/39 The Spores of Death
19. 06/19/39 The Spores of Death
20. 06/21/39 The Knocking on the Door
21. 06/23/39 The Knocking on the Door
22. 06/26/39 The Traveler from Tibet
23. 06/28/39 The Flower of Silence
24. 06/30/39 The Si-Fan Move
25. 07/03/39 Zarmi of the Joy Shop
26. 07/05/39 The Talun-Nar Chest
27. 07/07/39 The Golden Pomegranates
28. 07/10/39 A Midnight Summons
29. 07/12/39 The Cry of a Nighthawk
30. 07/14/39 Under the Elms
31. 07/17/39 Enter Mr. Abel Slattin
32. 07/19/39 The Climber
33. 07/21/39 The White Peacock
34. 07/24/39 Dark Eyes Look into Mine
35. 07/26/39 The Coughing Horror
36. 07/28/39 The Questing Hands
37. 07/30/39 The Silver Buddha
38. 08/02/39 The Bells
39. 08/04/39 The Six Gates

If collectors of the recordings were to accept "collector titles," they would have to understand that each of the extant recordings have as many as four different titles. Broadcast dates are also futile in the collecting world since the program aired in syndicated for-

Full page advertisements in *Broadcasting* magazine from 1938 and 1939, promoting *The Shadow of Fu Manchu* discs to radio station managers.

Full page advertisements in *Broadcasting* magazine from 1938 and 1939, promoting *The Shadow of Fu Manchu* discs to radio station managers.

Full page advertisements in *Broadcasting* magazine from 1938 and 1939, promoting *The Shadow of Fu Manchu* discs to radio station managers.

mat across the country on various dates. The most commonly accepted broadcast dates, for those who prefer to catalog their recordings with broadcast dates, are those from New York City when the program aired three days a week beginning on Monday, March 18, 1940. The best way to collect the recordings, however, is by episode number and the title of the novel from which they were adapted.

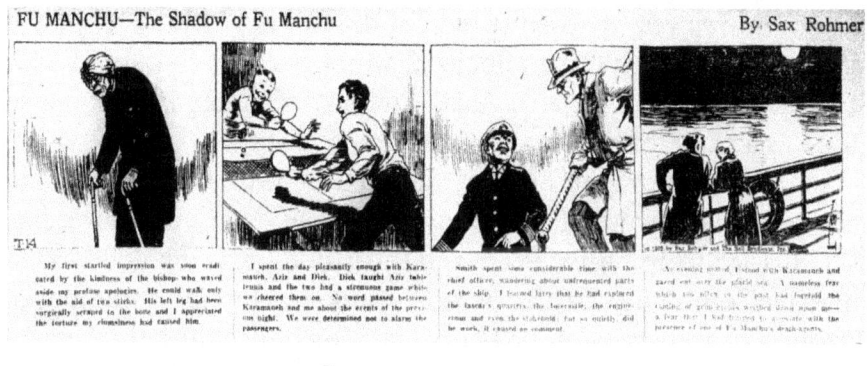

The Shadow of Fu Manchu newspaper strip as it appeared in *The Brooklyn Citizen* in October 1932.

ODDS AND ENDS

The death of 89-year-old Mitsuru Toyama in Tokyo on October 5, 1944, raised the question whether Dr. Fu Manchu was a fictional character... or so wrote a columnist for the *Chicago Daily News*. Toyama was chief of the Black Dragon Society, which frequently ruled Japan by intrigue and the murder of politicians who dared to defy its jingoistic aims. Toyama, sometimes spoken of as "unofficial Emperor," devoted himself to the "elimination of the red-haired barbarians" from East Asia for nearly 50 years.

As early as 1899 he was actively plotting against the United States with leaders of the Philippine Insurrection, including Emilio Aguinaldo. Among his later satellites were the puppet Chinese leader Wang Ching-Wei and Subhas Chandra Bose, head of the "Free India" movement. Before the turn of the century Toyama operated through the "Black Ocean Society," which was closely tied in with the "Association of Eastern Asia," a phony trade organization also used as a front for the Japanese system.

The Black Dragon Society, founded in 1901 by Toyama, had about 12,000 devoted fanatics enrolled. It was very exclusive, like the Russian Communist Party and the inside Nazi ring. It operated like the Communist parties of most countries through a number of "front" or "transmission belt" organizations, including the Society for Existence in the East, the Brigade for Combating Bolshevization of Great Japan, and the Red Swastika. The Celestial Salvation for the Oppressed was the Korean arm of Toyama, but it later branched into the Phillippines. Religion was take care of by the Doin Society, which sought to amalgamate Taoism, Buddhism, Mehammedanism, Christianity, Confucianism and other creeds.

The known life of this old enemy of America was so weird that it matched the wildest fiction of the Yellow Peril school of story writers.

WHITE VELVET

Sax Rohmer's other work on the printed page included supernatural horror and adventure in the Orient, from short stories to novels. Some of these were adapted into radio dramas. Following the publication of *President Fu Manchu* in 1936, Rohmer began work on a screenplay. It was set in Egypt and he created the scenario with Marlene Dietrich in mind. At least one of the Hollywood studios liked the proposed story and Rohmer was invited to go to Hollywood to complete the script and the sale. He never went; instead he wrote a novel and published in book form without the customary magazine serialization in advance. *White Velvet* concerned the investigation of dope smuggling in Egypt. The British secret service agent falls in love with the suspect, who clears herself by supplying him with information about the gang's activities. Rohmer's stock-in-trade of jeweled daggers, hashish, sliding doors, collapsing rooms and enigmatic Orientals were commonplace in the underworld of Port Said, as the hero sought drug-smugglers and jewel thieves.

The novel was printed in the February 21, 1937 issue of *The Philadelphia Inquirer*, with highlights of the story broadcast over radio stations WIP and WFIL on Saturday evening, February 27, 1937. This was part of an ongoing series at the time with the paper reprinting a novel in every Sunday paper, with highlights from the weekly novel adapted for local radio on the following Saturday.

Rohmer himself adapted the novel for a radio serial, broadcast over the BBC from April 29 to July 1, 1940. Howard Rose produced.

Episode #1, "The Big Four" (April 29, 1940)
Episode #2, "The Scarab Brooch" (May 6, 1940)
Episode #3, "The Port Said Customhouse" (May 13, 1940)
Episode #4, "The Apthorpe Diamonds" (May 20, 1940)
Episode #5, "The Port Said Tragedy" (May 27, 1940)
Episode #6, "Tabrer's Discovery" (June 3, 1940)
Episode #7, "The Song of Fate" (June 10, 1940)
Episode #8, "The Villa Malados" (June 17, 1940)
Episode #9, "In a Turkish Garden" (June 24, 1940)
Episode #10, "Musette Sings Again" (July 1, 1940)

CAST: Ivor Barnard (Kaspar), Dora Barton (Ma Koffman), Laidman Browne (Mahammed *and* Captain Shand), D.A. Clarke-Smith (Faramy Bey), Cathleen Cordell (Musette), Cherry Cotrell (Sally), Helen Crerar (Fuzzy), Philip Cunningham (Juan *and* the Arab), Valentine Dyall (Lawrence Tabrer), Neville Gates (Wally), Malcolm Graeme (Hogan), Betty Hardy (Sitka), Charles Mason (telephonist #2 *and* Ali), Edgar Norfolk (the stage manager *and* the second officer), Fred O'Donovan (telephonist #1), Leslie Perrins (Malagos), Bryan Powley (Abdul Akbar), Ivan Samson (Bruce Grimstone), Harold Scott (Nubian *and* Mabrouk), Ronald Simpson (Hawkins *and* the manager *and* Kingswood), William Trent (Lancaster), Ralph Truman (Pa Koffman), and Alan Wheatley (Kaspar). Also in the cast: Anne Firth and Mary O'Farrell.

The hero, Lawrence Tabrer, was played by actor Valentine Dyall, whose subsequent career included service as "The Man in Black," the host of a series of creepy mysteries scripted by John Dickson Carr, on a weekly radio series of the same name. One of the villains in the *White Velvet* radio serial, Faramy Bey, was played by D.A. Clarke-Smith, whose name appears earlier in this essay. Clarke-Smith played major roles in the stage productions of Rohmer's *The Eye of Siva* and *Secret Egypt*, and played the role of Nayland Smith in the Radio Luxembourg *Fu Manchu* serial. Actress Cathleen Cordell was better known as a screen actress than a radio actress and her appearance on this radio serial was through permission of British National Films, Ltd., and Pascall Film Productions, Ltd., as revealed by the radio announcer at the close of each broadcast.

THE ADVENTURES OF SUMURU

Second to Fu Manchu was Rohmer's other creation, the villainous Sumuru, a female counterpart that would become the central character in a series of five novels from 1950 to 1956.

After the end of World War II, Rohmer was approached by a representative of the BBC to write an adventure serial. Rohmer's initial intention was to bring Fu Manchu to British airwaves, but he was reminded of the network's policy against offending the Republic of China, Britain's ally in the war. Rohmer recycled the same basic plots from his prior Fu Manchu stories and changed the sex of the villain to a female mastermind named Sumuru.

The Shadow of Sumuru was broadcast in eight half-hour weekly installments from December 30, 1945 to February 17, 1946. The cast included Anna Burden (Sumuru), Anne Cullen (Claudette), Dorothy Gordon (Jean), Ralph Truman (Dr. Maitland), Robert Beatty (Mark Donovan), Lewis Stringer (Ian Forrester), Philip Cunningham (Ariosto), Arthur Bush (Inspector Ives), Patric Curwen (Colonel Stayton), Jane Howard (the nurse), Leslie Perrins (Caspar), Richard Wattis (Det. Sgt. Locker), and Arthur Young (Dr. Arlington), George Merrett (Philo).

In 1950, Rohmer adapted his radio serial into a novel, *The Sins of Sumuru*, later published in America under the title *Nude in Mink*. Like her criminal mastermind forerunner Dr. Fu Manchu, the beautiful Sumuru led a secret organization aimed at taking control of the world. Sumuru's society, the Order of Our Lady, recruited beautiful women to seduce and exploit men in order to establish a matriarchal world order. Sumuru was described as "a glamorous witch of totally untraceable nationality, heading an international crime organization which employed strange and bizarre devices."

Produced and directed by Noel Iliff, the radio serial does not exist in recorded form. Fans of Sax Rohmer wanting to know the plots of the eight installments need only read the first *Sumuru* novel for a faithful adaptation from the radio scripts.

> Episode #1, "The Green Sapphire" (December 30, 1945)
> Episode #2, "Tears of a Day" (January 6, 1946)
> Episode #3, "The Dumb Man" (January 13, 1946)
> Episode #4, "The Sleep-Walker" (January 20, 1946)
> Episode #5, "A Statue of Hamlet" (January 27, 1946)
> Episode #6, "Serpent Woman" (February 3, 1946)
> Episode #7, "The Tapping Stick" (February 10, 1946)
> Episode #8, "The Shadow Passes" (February 17, 1946)

The plot, as detailed in the novel, concerns Sumuru using sex to create hopeless male slaves, abducted and brainwashed, courtesy of beautiful women who hypnotize men into doing her will. Her goal is to establish a global dictatorship with herself as queen bee, making the world a beautiful place through forced breeding of good-looking intelligent people. "By mating beauty with genius, hope to produce a super race, a race with fine brains in fine bodies." One almost wonders if the sex was toned down for the radio rendition, and the fact that Sax Rohmer never adapted the serial into a novel until a few years after broadcast suggested he was eager to produce a quick novel out of financial necessity.

THE (ATTEMPTED) RETURN OF DR. FU MANCHU

As for future attempts to bring Fu Manchu back to American network radio, the following news blurb can be found in the January 29, 1946 issue of *Radio Daily*: "Another show for a strong comeback

Art work from a fan of old-time radio's *The Shadow* and *The Shadow of Fu Manchu*.

is *Dr. Fu Manchu*, being peddled by Colwell-Green with Otto Kruger in the title role." This reported attempt never met fruition.

The March 21, 1951 issue of *Variety* reported: "Herbert Bayard Swope, Jr., NBC-TV producer-director, has acquired the rights to all properties of Sax Rohmer, creator of Dr. Fu Manchu, and will use them as basis of several AM and TV series. NBC will get first crack at the programs. Wyllis Cooper is associated with Swope on the projected airers and will adapt the Rohmer stories. Shows in preparation include *Fu Manchu* and *Sax Rohmer Presents*, latter featuring the author as narrator of his short stories." The trade's reference to "AM" at the time meant radio. No radio pilot is known to have been produced in April 1952, but an unaired television pilot was filmed by Swope with Sir Cedric Hardwicke as Inspector Nayland Smith, and John Carradine as Dr. Fu Manchu. The proposed television series was supposedly the third in a series for NBC made specifically for television, along with *Dangerous Assignment* and *Tales of the Texas Rangers*, both of which did become weekly television programs. The network planned on adding the *Fu Manchu* program to its immediate syndication roster, months later, but accidentally permitted its option on the property to lapse after the pilot was completed. Robert Sarnoff, head of the NBC syndication operation, and other web brass, were disappointed in the pilot entry and decided to write off the approximate $20,000 expense rather than splurge to the tune of $750,000, the amount required for a 39-week cycle, on "a dubious entry."

On the evening of August 4, 1955, Sax Rohmer was among the numerous guest stars on *Show People*, broadcast over the BBC. In a special tribute to George Robey, comedian and singer of the English stage, who passed away months prior, a number of friends and associates took time to recount their friendship with the actor. Back in 1922, Robey starred in *Round in Fifty*, a modernized version of *Around the World in Eighty Days*, written by Sax Rohmer and Julian and Laurie Wylie. This was a personal favorite of the comedian, which ran for an impressive total of 471 performances. Rohmer recounted those good old days for the radio special.

The final appearance of Dr. Fu Manchu on radio was in the form of comedic spoof. On the evening of October 25, 1955, the weekly BBC radio program, *The Goon Show*, a comedy sketch program starring Peter Sellers, Harry Secombe and Spike Milligan, featured a sketch titled "The Terrible Revenge of Fred Fu Manchu." Years later, Peter Sellers would play the title role in a motion-picture, *The Fiendish Plot of Dr. Fu Manchu*, released in 1980. It would mark Seller's final screen appearance, having died two weeks before the movie premiere. Throughout the film, Fu Manchu asked his friends to call him "Fred."

THE MOLLÉ MYSTERY THEATRE

The highlight of this book is the script reprint of the 1944 radio broadcast of *Mollé Mystery Theatre*, an adaptation of one of Rohmer's novels. A recording of this broadcast is not known to exist. While the history of Sax Rohmer's literary work as it was adapted for radio drama is covered in this book chronologically, documentation of the 1944 radio broadcast is deliberately out of sequence and provided at the end of this book to introduce the radio script.

The final Fu Manchu radio broadcast was a one-time presentation on *The Mollé Mystery Theatre*, an anthology of mystery whodunits, sponsored by Cummer Products. Due to "skillful scripting and imaginative production," adequately described by *Variety* magazine, the weekly program successfully ran for more than a decade. The program featured the best in mystery and detective stories, adaptations of short stories, stage plays and novels written by such stalwarts as Raymond Chandler, Jack London, Cornell Woolrich, Robert Bloch, Earl Derr Biggers, Edgar Wallace, W.W. Jacobs, Rufus King, and Craig Rice.

On the evening of Tuesday, October 3, 1944, from 9 to 9:30 p.m. Eastern, the 1913 novel *The Insidious Dr. Fu Manchu* was dramatized, originating from NBC studios in New York. The program was narrated by famed criminologist Geoffrey Barnes, the on-the-air pseudonym of actor Roc Rogers (who was replaced by Bernard Lenrow as Barnes on the *Mollé Mystery Theatre* program in the fall of 1945). Jack Miller supplied the music. A number of publications and websites incorrectly list this episode with an August 22, 1944 broadcast date. The reason for confusion is because newspapers originally reported an adaptation of the Rohmer novel to be presented on that evening, courtesy of a press release.

Broadcast on the evening of August 22 was *The Case of the Talking Pills*, the second in a series of Jonathan Pierce mysteries, originally co-written for the radio program by Ken Crossen and H.L. Gold. *The Insidious Dr. Fu Manchu* was rescheduled for the evening of October 3.

CAST: Brad Barker (assorted sounds including the wail); Tony Barrett (Dr. Furneau); Horace Braham (Nayland Smith); Peter Cappel (Dr. Fu Manchu); Burford Hampden (Inspector Weymouth); John Moore (Dr. Petrie); Roc Rogers (Dr. Barnes); and Gloria Sturgis (Karamaneh).

The Host: Roc Rogers (as Geoffrey Barnes)
Announcer: Dan Seymour
Music: Jack Miller

> 7:45—WIL, Dance Time.
> 7:55—KMOX, Bill Henry, comment.
> **8 P. M.**
> KSD—Mystery Theater: "Dr Fu Manchu". KMOX, Burns and Allen Show. KWK, Gabriel Heatter. WIL, Scores; Music by the Bookful. KXOK, Famous Jury Trials.
> 8:15 — KWK, Screentest. WIL, Unity Viewpoint.

Verification in an October 3, 1944 newspaper that the Fu Manchu story was broadcast on October 3, 1944.

The Mollé Mystery Theatre
"Fu Manchu"

MARTIN

NBC   THE MOLLE MYSTERY THEATRE   (REVISED)
"FU MANCHU"
9:00 - 9:30 PM   OCTOBER 3, 1944   TUESDAY

ANNCR: Molle- M-O-L-L-E--(MUSIC SPELLING)- Molle, the brushless shaving cream with the special protective film that guards your face, presents the MOLLE MYSTERY THEATRE!

(MUSIC: _ _ MOLLE MYSTERY THEME . . . . DOWN BEHIND)

ANNCR: Tonight....Molle....the brushless shaving cream which puts face protection first-- brings you another in a series of programs which puts mystery and excitement first. Each Tuesday night at this time you hear one of the great mystery stories selected either from the famous classics or from the best of the moderns by Mr Geoffrey Barnes. Mr Barnes, having made a lifelong study of mystery fiction, is a connoisseur of fine detective stories.....Mr Barnes.

(MUSIC: _ _ SNEAK, SUSPENSE:) _

BARNES: Good evening, ladies and gentlemen, and welcome to THE MOLLE MYSTERY THEATRE.

Tonight we present an old fashioned but classic story of mystery and suspense centering around that world-famous oriental villain of mystery fiction.....Dr Fu Manchu...as created by Sax Rohmer. For over a quarter of a century now millions of mystery fans have followed the incredible adventures of Nayland Smith of Scotland Yard and his friend Dr Petrie, as they have pitted their skills against this cunning arch genius of crime. And once again tonight they meet their match. "THE INSIDIOUS DR FU MANCHU!"

-2-

(MUSIC: THEME ... AND OUT)

BARNES: Now before our play begins, listen-- listen to the sound of a weapon <u>fired</u> at our men by the enemy but <u>aimed</u> by someone here in America who talked too much.

(RIFLE BULLET RICHOCHET)

BARNES: Yes, Americans...when someone here at home talks carelessly it helps the enemy aim his guns at our men. So, don't <u>you</u> be that someone. If you know any war secret that has not been reported on the radio or in the newspapers, keep it a secret and help keep our men alive. And now tonight's play "The Insidious Dr Fu Manchu".

(MUSIC: STING ... INTO OMINOUS, ORIENTAL FU MANCHU THEME)

PETRIE: (CALMLY) I suppose it is difficult for you Americans comfortable in your homes across the ocean, to believe in the existence of the diabolic Dr Fu Manchu. But I-- Dr Petrie -- I can assure you that he does exist. I <u>know</u> he exists; I have seen him....a tall, lean, and sepulchral man...with a clean-shaven skull....a cruel, stone-like face.....and slanting cat-green eyes that eat through you like acid. I've actually heard Dr Fu Manchu speak....

FU MANCHU: Yes, this is my temporary laboratory, gentlemen. Quite a collection of poison fungi....and disease bacilli unknown to you Westerners...and over there...pythons.

(MUSIC: STING)

PETRIE: And I myself have sat terrified in the stillness of a dark room watching one of Dr Fu Manchu's creatures of death come crawling toward me...

(MUSIC: STING)

```
PETRIE:     And outside my window again and again, that terrible
            wail...the signal wail of a dacoit-- Those oriental
            killers who served Dr. Fu Manchu ---
VOICE:      (DISTANT, HIGH PITCHED WAIL...NOT QUITE HUMAN....)
(MUSIC:     _ _ CLIMATIC_STRAIN _ _UP AND OUT SHARP)_
PETRIE:     But to go back to the beginning....(PAUSE) I was sitting
            one winter's night in my London quarters, reading a
            chapter in Dickens' Martin Chuzzlewit when suddenly----
            (URGENT KNOCKS ON DOOR, SLIGHTLY OFF...DOOR BURST
            OPEN)
PETRIE:     Oh, it's you, Nayland.
            (DOOR SLAM, SLIGHTLY OFF)
NAYLAND:    (FADING ON) Sorry, Petrie, to break in on you like this
            but I need your help. Desperately!
PETRIE:     Now, Nayland. I'm in my slippers.....
NAYLAND:    It's a murder case, Petrie.
PETRIE:     Murder? Who?
NAYLAND:    .......... Jules Furneau...
PETRIE:     Jules Furneau?
            The famous explorer, just returned to England from a
            long trip to Tibet.                            (FADE)
                                                          it
FURNEAU:    (........PAIN GASPING VOICE) Hello...hello. Are
            you......?
```

-4-

NAYLAND: Speak up, man. I can scarcely hear you.
FURNEAU: Nayland...Nayland Smith?
NAYLAND: Yes? (PAUSE) What is it? What's wrong?
VOICE: (THE DISTANT, HIGH-PITCHED WAIL,...TWICE)
NAYLAND: What was that? What was that scream I heard? Speak up, man.
FURNEAU: (GASPING) Zayat...Zayat! Z-A-Y--
(ON FILTER...A GROAN, AND CRASH ONTO THE TELEPHONE)
NAYLAND: Hello....hello!
(RECEIVER JIGGLES)
NAYLAND: Hello! Are you there? (FADE) Mr. Furneau! Mr. Furneau! Hello! Hello! Mr. Furneau! (PAUSE) There was no answer....only a ghastly silence. I was more than mystified, Petrie. I was scared.
PETRIE: That word he tried to spell out...Zayat? What's --?
NAYLAND: That's what really unnerved me, Petrie. I'm certain Furneau was murdered while talking to me on the telephone!
PETRIE:
NAYLAND:
PETRIE:
NAYLAND: It means death....a horrible death! It also means that Dr Fu Manchu is here in London!

(MUSIC: _ _ EXCITING BRIDGE & HOLD)

-5-

PETRIE: I dressed as rapidly as I could, and accompanied Nayland Smith to the hotel where ~~turned toward the telephone call from~~ Jules Furneau. *stayed.* There we found the body slumped over the telephone, and, immediately sent the hotel (FADE) manager out to call Inspector Weymouth. *(STEPS)*

NAYLAND: Just as I suspected, Petrie. Look at the peculiar mark here on the back of the right hand.

PETRIE: Yes...Stange, isn't it? Like the print of red painted lips.

NAYLAND: That's it. The Zayat Kiss.

PETRIE: The Jazat Kiss!? ~~Nayland, what are you talking about?~~

NAYLAND: It's one of Dr Fu Manchu's favorite methods of murder. (~~NB SNIFFS~~) Do you smell anything, Petrie?

PETRIE: (~~SNIFFS~~) Yes...some kind of strong perfume...or flower scent.

NAYLAND: A kind you seldom find in Europe. And it's coming from this desk here, Petrie. From this blank envelope. Smell it.

PETRIE: (SNIFFS) Ah, yes.

(PAPER RUSTLE)

NAYLAND: And nothing in the envelope but a blank piece of paper. Wait a minute, Petrie! (FADING) *(STEPS)* Yes, just as I thought....

PETRIE: What did you find now, Nayland?

NAYLAND: (SLIGHTLY OFF) Come. Look for yourself. *(STEPS)*

PETRIE: A long piece of red silk thread....

NAYLAND: (ON) Hanging down the chimney. I was right. I know now exactly how Jules Furneau was murdered.

PETRIE: How?

-6-

NAYLAND: I'll explain later. Right now we must warn two other gentlemen, or we're likely to have two more murders.

PETRIE: Two more?

NAYLAND: Sir Crichton Davey and Lord Southery. They accompanied Jules Furneau on his trip to Tibet and returned to London with him a week ago.

(TELEPHONE RING)

PETRIE: Now what?

NAYLAND: Just a moment, Nayland! I'll answer it!

(TELEPHONE RING IS INTERRUPTED BY RECEIVER LIFT)

NAYLAND: Hello....This is Nayland Smith speaking....Oh, hello, Inspector Weymouth. Did you get my message?....What? What's that?!...Where?....Yes, yes, I'll be right over. I'll meet you there.

(HANG UP RECEIVER)

PETRIE: (FRIGHTENED) Nayland, what's happened?

NAYLAND: Sir Crichton Davey has been....murdered!

(MUSIC: DRAMATIC CHORD INTO BRIDGE)

PETRIE: Nayland Smith and I caught a cab and drove through the thick London fog to the suite of rooms occupied by Sir Crichton Davey. (FADE) There we met Inspector Weymouth.

WEYMOUTH: Here's Sir Crichton's body, Mr Smith.....just like I found him....lying all twisted up on the couch.

NAYLAND: I see (PAUSE)

PETRIE: (LOW) A horrible sight!

WEYMOUTH: Yes, sir.

NAYLAND: How much do you know about this, Weymouth?

-7-

WEYMOUTH: Well, according to Mr Burboyne...he's Sir Crichton's personal secretary...at 10 o'clock tonight Sir Crichton was in here writing at that table there by the fireplace...

NAYLAND: Yes?

WEYMOUTH: And at about 10:25 a messenger delivered this envelope I found on the table. Here it is, sir.

(RUSTLE OF PAPER)

NAYLAND: A blank envelope....and a blank piece of paper inside.

WEYMOUTH: Yes, sir.

PETRIE: That strange perfume, Nayland! It's the same perfume we found before.

NAYLAND: Yes, Petrie. Anything else, Weymouth?

WEYMOUTH: Well, sir, toward 11 o'clock Mr Burboyne heard a scream. He rushed in here and found Sir Crichton sprawled on that couch. He was gasping and saying something about a kiss.

PETRIE: The Zayat kiss!

NAYLAND: Exactly!

WEYMOUTH: I don't understand, Mr Smith.

NAYLAND: Never mind, Weymouth. Petrie, telephone the Explorers' Club, tell them it's an emergency...find out where Lord Southery lives, and then rush to him and tell him to go into hiding at once if he values his life!

PETRIE: Yes, Nayland. You mean Fu Manchu - - -

NAYLAND: Undoubtedly! I'll meet you back in your apartment within the next hour.

(MUSIC: _ _ STING_INTO B.G.)

-8-

PETRIE: Well, I found Lord Southery...warned him...and had some trouble in convincing him that he should go into hiding. But he promised to do so. Then I returned to my apartment.

(DISTANT CHIMES OF BIG BEN)

PETRIE: Just at midnight I was pacing up and down my room trying to piece together all the factors in this new Dr. Fu Manchu mystery...when

(KNOCK)

A little trembling I answered the door.

(DOOR OPEN)

KARAMANEH: You...you are Dr. Petrie?

PETRIE: Yes, I am. Won't you come in?

KARAMANEH: No, I cannot. I have been asked only to give you this envelope.

PETRIE: Oh.

KARAMANEH: You will yourself give it to Mr. Nayland Smith?

PETRIE: Certainly. I'll be glad to do that. But....but who are you?

KARAMANEH: That does not matter. But you -- you are a doctor. For a young man who has been hurt......who is sick. You could help him?

PETRIE: Who is it --- who is sick?

KARAMANEH: My brother. He is a prisoner of ---

PETRIE: A prisoner   I don't understand.

KARAMANEH: I can't explain now. When you give this envelope to Mr. Smith....leave him at once! Do not go near him any more tonight! Go away swiftly! Please! (FADE) Now, goodbye ......Dr. Petrie.

-9-

PETRIE: But I say! (CALLING) Wait! Wait a minute!
(MUSIC: _ _ PUNCTUATION)_
PETRIE: She disappeared down the hall, into the shadows. She was so beautiful, so exotic, that for a few moments I forgot all about the envelope she had given me. Then suddenly I was aware of a strange, heavy odor. I went white with fear. It was the same perfume I had smelled before at Jules Furneau's! I looked down at the envelope. It was blank.

(RUSTLE OF PAPER)

I opened it! It contained nothing but a blank sheet of paper...reeking with that eastern perfume!

(MUSIC: _ _ STING, SEVERAL TIMES AND OUT SHARP)_
NAYLAND: Yes, I have heard of the girl, Petrie. Her name is Karamaneh. Perhaps one of the finest weapons in Dr. Fu Manchu's armory.
PETRIE: Oh, I see. But this envelope...why was it been sent to you? How did she know our names?
NAYLAND: ~~[crossed out]~~

VOICE: (THE HIGH-PITCHED WAIL AGAIN...)
PETRIE: (STARTLED) What's that?
NAYLAND: (TENSE) That's the cry of a dacoit!
PETRIE: A what?
NAYLAND: A dacoit. We're being closed in upon by the most dangerous killer the world has ever known!
PETRIE: You mean Dr. Fu Manchu---!

-10-

NAYLAND: Yes. We've tried to interfere with his plot...now he's determined to get rid of us...

PETRIE: Good Lord, Nayland! Not--!

NAYLAND: We've got to make the best of this-- and I think we can succeed.

(RATTLE OF CLUBS IN GOLF BAG)

PETRIE: What are you doing in my golf bag?

NAYLAND: This driver is just the thing. I think it'll turn the trick.

VOICE: (THE WAIL AGAIN....)

NAYLAND: Quick! Turn out the lights.

(SNAP OF LIGHT SWITCH)

NAYLAND: (LOW) Now, Petrie, we'll put this scented envelope here on this table by the open window....

PETRIE: (LOW) But, Nayland, I still don't----!

NAYLAND: Now come over here in the shadows and sit by me. (PAUSE) Everything's all right, Petrie. All right. I expect a visitor very shortly.

(SNEAK CLOCK TICKING IN)

(TENSE PAUSE)

PETRIE: The young lady?

NAYLAND: (LOW) No, Petrie. And keep your voice down!

(TENSE PAUSE...CLOCK TICKING)

PETRIE: (LOW) But who is the girl? Do you know?

NAYLAND: Either Dr. Fu Manchu's wife, daughter or slave. My guess is that she's a slave.

PETRIE: What a horrible life for a---!

-11-

NAYLAND: Keep your eye on the open window, and I think you'll learn how the Zayat kiss works.

VOICE: ~~(THE MAIL AGAIN)~~

~~(A TENSE PAUSE)~~

PETRIE: The Zayat kiss...What does it mean, Nayland?

NAYLAND: (LOW) Zayats are rest houses in Tibet. And travellers ~~have stopped at these houses~~ have died, with nothing to show as the cause of their deaths but a small red mark on the face. The ~~same kind of~~ mark ~~was~~ on Jules Furneau and Sir Crichton. It's called the Zayat kiss.

PETRIE: And the heavy perfume on the envelope and blank paper?

NAYLAND: From a green orchid that grows in the swampy forests of Tibet. It gives off a pungent odor that attracts the creatures.

PETRIE: Creatures!!?

(RUSTLE OF VINES...SCRAPING OF WOOD...SLIGHTLY OFF AND UNDER)

NAYLAND: (QUICKLY) Quiet! Our visitor is now at the open window.

(MUSIC: SOFT CHORD, AND HOLD UNDER WITH THEME OF IMPENDING DANGER)

PETRIE: (LOW NARRATIVE) Smith and I sat motionless in the dark room...watching the fog come in the open window. And then, in the hall light, I saw a lithe, black-clad figure appear above the sill. Next I could make out a bony hand holding a small square box...There was a faint click, and the figure dropped away from the window. Then silence.

(PAUSE)

(MORE)

-12-

PETRIE: Then, when Nayland nudged me and pointed, I saw it on the
(CONT) table...running rapidly about the scented envelope...
vividly red and venomous...a giant scorpion!

(SEVERAL SHOTS..THEN THE SMASH OF THE GOLF CLUB
ON THE TABLE MANY TIMES)

NAYLAND: I got it, Petrie, I got it! Keep away from that window!

PETRIE: But that native outside...

NAYLAND: I'm afraid I missed him and we'll never catch him.
Turn on the lights.

(LIGHT SWITCH CLICK)

NAYLAND: There's your dead scorpion.

PETRIE: Ugh! What a horrible creature!

PETRIE: And this is what killed Sir Crichton and Jules Furneau?

NAYLAND: Exactly. A red scorpion like this one was lowered down
the chimneys by means of a silk thread.

(TELEPHONE RINGS)

PETRIE: I'll get it. (PHONE UP) Hello....Yes, this is Dr.
Petrie speaking...Oh, yes, Lord Southery...(LONG PAUSE)
What?!...No, no, Lord Southery. Stay where you are!....
Nayland Smith and I'll be over within ten minutes...
Yes. Goodbye.

(PHONE DOWN)

PETRIE: Lord Southery is afraid to leave his room. He's been
hearing a strange wailing outside his window!

NAYLAND: Petrie. We haven't a minute to lose!
Southery's life depends on our getting there in time.

(MUSIC: EXCITE)

-13-

	(...DOOR OPENS...DOOR CLOSES)	16.00
NAYLAND:	Right down this hallway, I guess.	
	(FOOTSTEPS IN HALLWAY)	
PETRIE:	Here we are -- fourth floor rear.	
	(KNOCK ON DOOR)	16.15
	(PAUSE)	
	(KNOCK ON DOOR....TWICE)	
NAYLAND:	Nobody seems to be in.	
PETRIE:	But he just telephoned us!	
NAYLAND:	I'll try the latch.	
PETRIE:	(LOW) Careful, Nayland!	
	(DOOR SLOWLY BEING OPENED)	
NAYLAND:	It's unlatched!	
	(PAUSE)	16.30
NAYLAND:	Nobody. Where's the light switch?	
	(SUDDEN THUD...SMITH GROANS...BODY FALLS TO FLOOR)	
PETRIE:	(STARTLED) Smith! Smith!	
	(REPEAT THUD...AND BODY FALLS TO FLOOR)	
FU MANCHU:	The fools! To think they can cope with Fu Manchu! (LAUGHS)	16.45
		17.00
	(MIDDLE CURTAIN)	

(Music Bridge)

MOLLE MYSTERY THEATRE -14-
"FU MANCHU" 10/3/44

FIRST COMMERCIAL:
14-26
BARNES: Well, Molle Mystery fans, you can see that Dr. Fu Manchu 17.20
is a very unpleasant character indeed. And I can assure
you that he doesn't get any more loveable as our play 17.30
goes along.

SEYMOUR: You said it, Mr. Barnes! He's the kind of gent that
something awful should happen to. Why...why...I'll even
go so far as to hope that he gets nicks and scrapes while
shaving every morning of his life.

BARNES: You mean you wouldn't sell him any Molle, Dan? 17.45

SEYMOUR: Exactly, Mr. Barnes. I'd just say to him. See here.
There are plenty of men who <u>deserve</u> the kind of shave
17-86
Molle gives...plenty of good men who need the face
protection you get when you shave with Molle Brushless
Shaving Cream. I'd say to him...let the other men put 18.00
face protection <u>first</u> with Molle's special protective
film. As for you....

(DISTANT CHINESE GONG)

SEYMOUR: (QUAKING IN BOOTS) Uh...uh uh...if that's Dr Fu Manchu,
I was only fooling.

(MUSIC:_ _ _ _CHORD IN G...SEGUE TO PROGRAM MUSIC)

SEYMOUR: (CHUCKLE) No fooling, friends, you <u>can</u> get swell, 18.15
comfortable shaves when you put <u>face protection</u> FIRST
18-27
with Molle. Now here is Mr. Barnes, with Act Two of
"The Insidious Dr. Fu Manchu"

(MUSIC:_ _ _ _UNDER) 18.30

-1-

BARNES: Dr. Petrie and Nayland Smith of Scotland Yard are on the trail of Dr. Fu Manchu, arch-criminal. Rushing to save the explorer, Lord Southery, Dr. Petrie and Smith are taken prisoner by Fu Manchu.

(FADE IN LIGHT RATTLE OF CHAINS)

NAYLAND: (GROANS)

PETRIE: (DAZED) Smith...is that you?

NAYLAND: (GROGGY) Right here.

PETRIE: What happened?

NAYLAND: Someone was in Lord Southery's...behind the door...and sandbagged us.

PETRIE: My head. Where are we?

NAYLAND: Chained in some sort of a dungeon.

(CHINESE GONG...OFF)

PETRIE: What's that?

(DOOR LOCK RATTLES...LIGHTLY OFF)

NAYLAND: Quiet! Someone's coming.

(IRON DOOR OPENED SLIGHTLY OFF...SOFT FOOTSTEPS FADE ON)

NAYLAND: (LOW) It's Dr. Fu Manchu!

(MUSIC: SHARP CHORD...HOLD UNDER)

FU MANCHU: (SLOW AND EVEN) Mr. Nayland Smith..and Dr. Petrie. It is most unfortunate, gentlemen, that you were fools enough to interfere with my mission here in London. You should have known better....You were planning to warn Lord Southery? Well, gentlemen, you have failed..Lord Southery is also my guest of honor. He's still alive-- for the moment.

NAYLAND: You fiend!

-16-

FU MANCHU: And as for you two gentlemen...I despise you for your bungling incompetence...for you stupid occidental minds. You must be prevented from ever interfering again. This is my temporary laboratory, gentlemen. Quite a collection of poison fungi, and disease bacilli unknown to you Westerners...and over here...pythons!

(MUSIC: _ _ _ _STING_AND_OUT)

(GONG)

PETRIE: Then Dr. Fu Manchu disappeared. Neither Nayland or I knew what fate to expect...or how soon it would come... We tried not to talk about it.

(LIGHT RATTLE OF CHAINS UNDER)

PETRIE: Nayland, what are you doing?

NAYLAND: I trying...to force the lock....on this chain...But I'm not succeeding.

(A DULL THUD...AND A SCRAPING OF STONE....AS A TRAP DOOR OPENS SLOWLY OFF UNDER)

NAYLAND: Look, Petrie, look! A trap door in the floor!

PETRIE: It's opening! There's a weird light...

(MUSIC: _ _ _ _KARAMANAH THEME UNDER)

KARAMANAH: (LOW) Dr Petrie! Dr. Petrie!

NAYLAND: The slave girl. Karamanah!

PETRIE: (CALLING) Yes! What is it, Karamanah?

KARAMANAH: You must be quiet, or he will kill all of us! Here are the keys for the locks.

PETRIE: The keys But why are you doing this?

NAYLAND: It's a trick, Petrie. She's one of Fu Manchu's agents.

-17-

KARAMANEH:	Yes, but only because Dr. Fu Manchu holds my brother prisoner. I want to help you escape so you can return and rescue my brother.
NAYLAND:	All right then. Just tell us how to get out of here.
KARAMANEH:	Go thru the trap door. Below there is a passage that will take you to the river. You can find it easily.
PETRIE:	And you?
KARAMANEH:	I must leave you now.
PETRIE:	No, Karamaneh. Come with us.
KARAMANEH:	I cannot. (FADE) Goodbye and good luck.
PETRIE:	Karamaneh! Wait!
NAYLAND:	She's gone, Petrie! And we better get going ourselves. As soon as we get out of here, we'll call Inspector Weymouth and a squad of men from Scotland Yard, and surround the place. We must get Dr. Fu Manchu dead or alive!

(MUSIC: _ _ _ EXCITE)

(DISTANT BOAT WHISTLES..FOG HORN)

NAYLAND:	This is the entrance, gentlemen.
WEYMOUTH:	(LOW) Huh...an old East End warehouse.
PETRIE:	How about your men, Inspector Weymouth?
WEYMOUTH:	The building's completely surrounded, Dr. Petrie.
NAYLAND:	I'm afraid..afraid something'll go wrong.
WEYMOUTH:	No, Mr. Smith!
NAYLAND:	But we've got to take the chance! We've got to break into the place!

(MUSIC: _ _ _ _ DANGER THEME... AND UPTO)

(DOOR CRASH IN)

-18-

PETRIE:	Karamaneh! Are you all right?	22.4
KARAMANEH:	Yes, Dr. Petrie, and here on this cot is my brother, and the other gentlemen.	
NAYLAND:	Lord Southery! Lord Southery!	
PETRIE:	No use, Nayland, they're both dead.	
KARAMANEH:	No, they are not dead...only a living death. (PAUSE)	
NAYLAND:	Yes. An artificial catalepsy.	
WEYMOUTH:	▬▬▬▬▬	23.00
KARAMANEH:	I have the antidote, Dr. Petrie. I can revive them.	
WEYMOUTH:	Where's Dr. Fu Manchu?	
KARAMANEH:	He has gone. As soon as he heard that you, Mr. Smith and you, Dr. Petrie, had escaped..he disappeared.	
MANCHU:	(ON P.A. SYSTEM) (LAUGHS)	23.15
(MUSIC: _ _ _ UNDER)		
WEYMOUTH:	Blimey! What's that?	
NAYLAND:	It's Fu Manchu!	
WEYMOUTH:	But where? I can't see him.	
NAYLAND:	I know. His voice must be coming from some hidden loud speaker. Stand by for trouble, Inspector Weymouth! And shoot to kill!	
MANCHU:	(LAUGHS) Shoot to kill _what_, gentlemen? No, gentlemen, you are the ones who shall die -- like rats in a trap!	23.30
(MUSIC: _ _ _ STING AND OUT)		
	(STEEL PANEL..SLIDING)	
KARAMANEH:	Look -- that steel door -- stop it!	23.41
	(SOUND. COMPLETE)	

-19-

PETRIE: Nayland! Inspector! A **steel panel has slid across the doorway. Unless we can batter it down we're trapped!** Come on! Help me!

(SOUND: POUNDING AND AD LIBS OF MEN AT DOOR)

FU MANCHU: (LAUGHS)

NAYLAND: Wait! Hold it!

(SOUND: OUT)

NAYLAND: It's no use, men. We're trapped!

MANCHU: A very erudite observation, my dear Nayland Smith. Now, in just a moment this room will fill with poison gas. And as for me-- I have no trouble slipping thru your men surrounding the building. Good-bye, my friends

(COUGHING OF MEN....POUNDING ON DOOR)

AD LIB FROM ALL

-20-

PETRIE: Nayland! Wait!

(POUNDING STOPS)

NAYLAND: Yes, Petrie, what is it?

PETRIE: Isn't this the same room we were in before?

NAYLAND: By Jove, it is!

PETRIE: The trap door, then. We can get out the trap-door. Here, help me with it.

NAYLAND: Right!

(TUGGING AT DOOR AND AD LIB GRUNTS OF MEN)

NAYLAND: No use! It's locked. It won't budge.

KARAMANEH: Dr. Petrie, somewhere hidden in the wall is a spring. I've seen Dr. Fu Manchu push it. It opens the trap-door.

NAYLAND: Hidden in the wall? Where? The wall is smooth as glass.

KARAMANEH: (COUGHS) I think I can find it. The spring is hidden about---(GROANS)---the gas---I---(FAINTS)

PETRIE: Karamaneh! Karamaneh! She's fainted.

WEYLAND: Fainted? You must revive her Dr. Petrie...or we'll never find the hidden spring.

PETRIE: That's impossible! The only way to revive her is to get her out in the open.

NAYLAND: Never mind. We're wasting time. We must find the spring ourselves.

WEYLAND: Right. She started for the wall here. If we go over it carefully with our fingers---

-21-

NAYLAND: (COUGH) That's the idea. Let's go...
(PAUSE...MEN'S FEET AS THEY MOVE ABOUT)

WEYLAND: (COUGH) Any luck?

SMITH: None, inspector. How about you, Nayland?

NAYLAND: Nothing. If there's a secret spring here, it's hidden devilishly well.

SMITH: I have an idea. The portion containing the spring must be more hollow than the rest of the wall.

WEYLAND: We better work fast. We can't stand this much longer.

NAYLAND: (COUGH) I know. Look. Let's be systematic. Inspector, you take the base of the wall. Petrie, you the left and I'll take the right. Now, get busy.

WEYMOUTH: Right you are!

(SOUND: TAPPING ON SOLID SURFACE FOR A MOMENT THEN:)

WEYLAND: Dr. Petrie, Nyland...it's no use...the gas...I...(FAINTS)

(SOUND: BODY FALL)

PETRIE: Help me with him, Nayland.

NAYLAND: Never mind. (WEAKLY) The only way to help him is to get out of here. (COUGHS) Keep tapping, Petrie.

(TAPPING A MOMENT, THEN:)

NALAND: Petrie...Petrie....I...(FAINTS)

-22-

PETRIE

Nayland! (COUGHS) Now, it's up to me.... 27.00
(GETS WEAKER) I must find that spring....
must get the trap-door open...

(TAPPING IS UNDER FROM "KEEP TAPPING" ABOVE...ON SOLID
SURFACE..AT THIS POINT TAPPING HITS HOLLOW SURFACE)
(STOPS ABRUPTLY WHEN HE HITS HOLLOW SURFACE) The
hollow part....(TAPS)....That's it...(TAPS)... 27.11
It must be ..(VERY WEAK)...Now if I can just touch
the secret spring... Ah, the spring...I can feel it
under my fingers...but why doesn't the trap-door open?
Why doesn't it....(GROANS AND FAINTS) 27.30

SOUND: BODY FALL....THEN SLOW CREAK AS TRAP DOOR OPENS

PAUSE

MUSIC AND DOWN INTO FOG-HORNS 27.50

PETRIE: Karamaneh....Karamaneh....

KARAMANEH: (GROANS)

NAYLAND: Is she all right, Petrie?

PETRIE: Yes, she's coming to? 28.00

KARAMANEH: (WEAKLY) What happened? Where are we?

PETRIE: We're outside. We all fainted from the gas, but
apparently I touched the hidden spring and opened the
trap-door. The fresh air revived Nayland and me and we
managed to drag you and Weymouth and Lord Southery and 28.15
your brother to safety.

-23-

KARAMANEH: My brother. Is he ---

PETRIE: Don't worry. He'll be all right. Nayland, what about Dr. Fu Manchu? ~~Do you~~ ~~managed to slip thru the men guarding the warehouse?~~

NAYLAND: Inspector Weymouth is questioning his men about that now...Oh, here he is! Any luck, Weymouth?

WEYMOUTH: (FADE IN) No, same old story, I'm afraid. None of my men saw the devil.

~~He must be still in the warehouse.~~

WEYMOUTH: ~~~~ My men searched the place thoroughly. He's just disappeared...completely.

PETRIE: Well, then -- wherever he is, we'll find him. We must, Nayland. The world isn't safe with such a man alive.

NAYLAND: Well, some day, perhaps---somewhere and somehow--- my friend, we may yet rid the world of that fiendish criminal.. ~~~~ But I have my doubts.

I'm afraid Dr. Fu Manchu will continue to exist in the world---like the forces of evil, which he seems somehow to symbolize.

(MUSIC: CURTAIN)

MOLLE MYSTERY THEATRE
FU MANCHU 10/3/44
SECOND COMMERCIAL:

-24-

BARNES: Well, as you Molle mystery fans who are also Fu Manchu fans know...the insidious Doctor does come back...always. He's about as sure to come back as summertime...or as the tax collector, or...or...

SEYMOUR: Would you say, Mr. Barnes...as sure as that nick or scrape you're likely to get tomorrow if you nicked or scraped your face while shaving today?

BARNES: Exactly, Dan.

SEYMOUR: And you gentlemen know that's so, too. For instance, if, as you were shaving today, you nicked your face...like this --

(MUSIC: _ _ _ TWANG OF VIOLIN OR CELLO STRING)

SEYMOUR: Why, as you're shaving tomorrow...when your razor reaches the same place on your face you're likely to get another nick...like this --

(MUSIC: _ _ _ TWANG OF VIOLIN OR CELLO STRING)

SEYMOUR: So, that's why it's a good idea to put face protection FIRST by shaving with MOLLE (██████████████████ ███████████) the brushless shaving cream with the special protective film. Molle helps guard your skin from irritating little nicks and scrapes because, you see --

VOICE: MOLLE'S special film has more real body and substance than light, fluffy cream. It gives your razor something to ride on.

SEYMOUR: And then, also.......

-21-

SECOND COMMERCIAL (CONTD)

VOICE: MOLLE'S special film contains a blend of beard-softening ingredients and non-irritating oils that are actually of medical purity. MOLLE is made of official United States Pharmacopeia ingredients....the same as used to fill doctor's prescriptions.

SEYMOUR: Yes, in every way face protection comes FIRST when you use MOLLE. So, your first MOLLE shave is really pleasant. And day after day, as that special film helps guard your skin...your shaves get better (MUSIC)....better.... (MUSIC) and better...(MUSIC when you shave with M-O-L-L-E (MUSIC: FIVE NOTES) MOLLE, the brushless shaving cream that puts <u>face protection</u> FIRST.

-22-

(AFTER COMMERCIAL)
(MUSIC: _ _ _ SNEAK B.G.)
SEYMOUR: And now MN Barnes will tell you about the Molle Mystery Theatre's play for next week.
BARNES:

(MUSIC: _ _ _ THEME UP AND DOWN)
SEYMOUR: The original music for the Molle Mystery Theatre is composed and conducted by Jack Miller. "The Insidious Fu Manchu" was written by Sax Rohmer. Until next Tuesday this is Dan Seymour saying good night and good shaving with Molle (MUSIC) the Brushless Shaving Cream that puts face protection first.
(MUSIC: _ _ _ THEME UP TO FINISH)

BARNES: NEXT WEEK, LADIES AND GENTLEMEN, IT WILL BE OUR PLEASURE TO BRING YOU ONE OF THE WORLD'S OUTSTANDING DRAMATIC ACTRESSES---LOUISE RAINER. MISS RAINER WILL BE STARRED IN ETHEL LINA WHITE'S SUSPENSEFUL MYSTERY TALE "THE WHEEL SPINS" ON WHICH THE FAMOUS MOTION PICTURE "THE LADY VANISHES" WAS BASED. THIS ADVENTURE IN CRIME HAS BEEN ACCLAIMED ONE OF THE CLEVEREST THRILLERS OF ATMOSPHERIC MYSTERY----AND, I AM SURE, YOU WILL FIND OUR PRESENTATION OF THIS ABSORBING TALE VITAL ENTERTAINMENT.

SO, MYSTERY FANS, WE INVITE YOU TO BE WITH US, NEXT WEEK, FOR THE UNIQUE IN EXCITEMENT AND SUSPENSE, WHEN YOU MEET LOUISE RAINER IN: "THE WHEEL SPINS!".....

IRONIZED YEAST....
HITCH HIKE
                                                    (REVISED)
ANNCR: Every day -- thousands of men and women supplement their
diet with I.Y. -- Ironized Yeast Tablets. (SLIGHT PAUSE)
Is your diet deficient in IRON? Do you need more
VITAMIN B-ONE? I.Y. Tablets give you extra IRON....to
help build rich, red blood. Extra VITAMIN B-ONE....to
help keep nerves steady, help you maintain pep and
strength. (SLIGHT PAUSE) To help keep vigor and
vitality - take Ironized Yeast. They're small, easy-to-
swallow tablets. Insist on I.Y. -- Ironized Yeast
Tablets!

MUSIC TO ---

Index

Adventures of Ellery Queen, The (radio program) 43
Adventures of Pinocchio, The (radio program) 55
Adventures of Rin-Tin-Tin (radio program) 27-29
Adventures of Sherlock Holmes (movie) 9
Agin, Boyd 14
Around the World in Eighty Days (novel) 72
Arthur, Jack 16

Barker, Brad 74
Barnard, Ivor 68
Barnes, Geoffrey 73
Barrett, Tony 74
Barrison, Phil 16
Barton, Dora 68
Bean, Clifford 43-45
Beatty, Robert 69
Bell, Clephan 44
Bendtsen, France 14
Beutelle, Lenoa 20
Bianca in Black (book) 5
Biggers, Earl Derr 35, 73
Black Camel, The (novel) 35
Bloch, Robert 73
Braham, Horace 74
Breustedt, Pauline 14

Bride of Fu Manchu, The (novel) 59
Briney, Robert E. 6, 40
Broadcasting (magazine) 53, 62-64
Brooklyn Citizen, The (newspaper) 65
Browne, Herbert 43
Browne, Laidman 68
Burden, Anna 69
Burke, Patricia 45
Burt, Oliver 45
Bush, Arthur 69
Butcher, Fannie 25

Caldwell, Nate 31-34
Cappel, Peter 74
Cardew, Phil 44, 45
Carfax, Bruce 44
Carr, John Dickson 68
Carradine, John 72
Chandler, Raymond 73
Charlie Chan (radio program) 59
Chase, Adelaide 14
Chicago Daily News, The (newspaper) 65
Chicago Tribune, The (newspaper) 24
Chu-Chin-Chow (stage play) 38
Clarke-Smith, D.A. 39, 40, 45, 68, 69

Cochrane, Frank 38-40
Coldwell, Nate 11
Collier Hour, The (radio program) 14-22
Collier's (magazine) 14-17, 21, 23, 48
Columbus Dispatch, The (newspaper) 12, 56
Conner, Travis 6, 60
Conoco Adventures (radio program) 27
Cooper, Wyllis 71
Cordell, Cathleen 68, 69
Cotrell, Cherry 68
Count of Monte Cristo, The (radio program) 59
Crerar, Helen 68
Crimson Fang, The (radio program) 36
Crossen, Ken 73
Cullen, Anne 69
Cunningham, Philip 68, 69
Curwen, Patric 69

Daly, John C. 28, 29, 51
Daly, John Charles 29
Damai, Paul K. 23
Dangerous Assignment (television program) 72
Daniels, Bebe 44
Daughter of Fu Manchu, The (novel) 59
Daughter of the Dragon (movie) 4, 5, 21
Davenport, Ted 6, 59
David, Gilbert 45
Davis, Colonel 20
Davis, Peggy 31, 51
Day the World Ended, The (novel) 18, 19, 48
Day the World Ended, The (radio program) 18, 19

Dayton Daily News, The (newspaper) 12
De Wolff, Francis 44
Death at Broadcasting House (novel) 45
Democrat and Chronicle (newspaper) 16
Denham, Maurice 43, 45
Dennis, Ivor 44
Des Moines Register & Tribune (newspaper) 56
Dietrich, Marlene 66
Doc Savage, Man of Bronze (radio program) 73q
Dope: A Story of Chinatown (novel) 8
Drums of Fu Manchu, The (cliffhanger) 4, 49
Drums of Fu Manchu, The (novel) 59
Ducrow, Peter 44
Dyall, Valentine 68

Earle, Helen 27
Ella Cinders (radio program) 55
Emperor of America, The (novel) 5, 17, 18
Emperor of America, The (radio program) 17, 18
Empire Builders, The (radio program) 27, 28
Eno Crime Club (radio program) 29, 35
Ephraim, Lee 49
Erskine, Eileen 44
Erskine, John 16
Eyes of Siva, The (stage play) 39, 69

Famous Jury Trials (radio program) 74
Fennelly, Parker 20
Fields, Harry David 55

Fields, Norman 51
Fiendish Plot of Dr. Fu Manchu, The (movie) 72
First Nighter Program (radio program) 27, 33, 34, 49
Firth, Anne 68
Fiske, Robert 31, 51
Five Star Theater (radio program) 34, 35
Flash Gordon (comic strip) 47
Frankau, Ronald 45
Frayling, Christopher 6
French, Ken 54
Fu Manchu's Daughter (novel) 15, 16, 19

Gates, Neville 68
Ghost Train, The (novel) 44
Giffard, Pierre 7
Girl Reporter (radio program) 27
Gold, H.L. 73
Golden Scorpion, The (novel) 48
Goon Show, The (radio program) 72
Gordon, Dorothy 69
Gordon, Gale 51
Graeme, Malcolm 68
Graham, Robert 44
Great Adventure (radio program) 12, 13
Green Hornet, The (radio program) 35
Gynt, Greta 45

Hall, Cameron 40
Hampden, Burford 74
Hand of Fu Manchu, The (novel) 59
Hardwicke, Sir Cedric 72
Hardy, Betty 68
Harris, Vernon 44
Hatch, Ike 45
Hayes, Shelagh 20
Heatter, Gabriel 74

Henry, Bill 74
Hickerson, Jay 6
Hill, Ronald 45
Hobbs, Carleton 47
Hopalong Cassidy (radio program) 55
Hope, Doug 29
Howard, Jane 69
Huber, Harold 30
Hughes, Arthur 20
Hughes, Charles 34
Hughes, Spike 45

Ibbett, Frederick George 27, 28, 32, 51
Iliff, Noel 70
Indianapolis Star, The (newspaper) 23
Infernal War, The (novel) 7
Insidious Dr. Fu Manchu, The (novel) 2, 7, 25, 59, 73
Insidious Dr. Fu Manchu, The (radio broadcast) 11, 21, 22, 26, 31, 34, 35
Inspector Brookes of Scotland Yard (radio program) 42
Irving, Sir Henry 29
Irwin, Boyd 11
Ivans, Perry 14

Jack Armstrong, the All-American Boy (radio program) 28
Jacobs, W.W. 73
Johns, Glynis 39
Johns, Mervyn 39, 41
Johnson, Urban 27
Jones, Sammy 6
Just Plain Bill (radio program) 20

K-7: Secret Service Spy Story (radio program) 29
Karloff, Boris 4, 21, 32

Kelso, Vernon 39, 41
Kennedy, John B. 16, 21, 23
King, Margaret 51
King, Rufus 73
Kirkland, Muriel 14
Kruger, Otto 71

La Guerre Infernale (novel) 7
Lambert, Jack 40
LaPrade, Ernest 20
LaPrade, Malcolm 20
Lennick, David 6
Lewis, Jack 52
Lind, Janet 45
Lofts, W.O.G. 40
London, Jack 73
Lone Ranger, The (radio program) 35
Lone Wolf Tribe (radio program) 24
Louisville Courier-Journal, The (newspaper) 24
Love, Sunda 30, 31, 51
Loy, Myrna 19
Lyons, Harry Agar 9

Macdonald, Norman 29, 51
MacFadycan, Barbara 43
Manhunters-O-Fangs (radio program) 36
Mansfield, Richard 29
Manson, Charles 30
Marcelle, Lou 52
Marion-Crawford, Howard 44
Marshall, Robert 43
Martin-Harvey, Michael 49
Marx Brothers, The 34, 35
Marx, Groucho 35
Maschwitz, Eric 45
Mask of Fu Manchu, The (movie) 4, 19, 21, 33
Mask of Fu Manchu, The (novel) 59

Mason, Charles 68
Master of Sinister House (short story) 16
Master of Villainy (book) 5, 40
Matthews, Douglas 45
Maynard, William Patrick 6
McBryde, Jack 26
McDonald, C.C. 52
McLeod, Gordon 40
Merchant of Venice, The (stage play) 29
Merrett, George 69
Millar, Lee 51
Miller, David 44
Miller, Jack 73, 74
Milligan, Spike 72
Mohr, Gerald 51, 52
Molle Mystery Theatre, The (radio program) 73
Moncrieff, Murray 44
Moore, John 74
Morning Call, The (newspaper) 10
Morris, McKay 13
Motor Rally Mystery, The (novel) 43
Mour, Jerry 51
Munster Times, The (newspaper) 23
Music by the Bookful (radio program) 74
Myrt and Marge (radio program) 24, 28
Mysterious Dr. Fu Manchu, The (movie) 3, 13
Mystery of Dr. Fu Manchu, The (novel) 2, 7

Nelson, Frank 51
Nightingale, The (musical) 48, 49
Norfolk, Edgar 68
Nude in Mink (novel) 69

O'Brien, Edmund 51
O'Donovan, Fred 68

O'Farrell, Mary 44, 68
Oland, Warner 4, 13, 20
Oppenheim's E. Phillips 16
Orange Lantern, The (radio program) 26
Osborne, Theodore 51
Owen, William 31

Palmer, Arnold 54
Perrins, Leslie 68, 69
Philadelphia Inquirer, The (newspaper) 68
Pickeled Peppers (stage play) 31
Pierce, Jonathan 73
Pittsburgh Press, The (newspaper) 29
Pola, Eddie 39
Ports of Call (radio program) 52
Powley, Bryan 43, 45, 68
President of Fu Manchu, The (novel) 59, 66
Price, Hamilton 45
Purdell, Reginald 43

Quest of the Sacred Slipper, The (novel) 7, 38, 39
Quest, Bill 45

Radio Daily (periodical) 70
Radio Pictorial (magazine) 37
Rae, John 40
Randolph, Isabel 31, 51
Rendel, Hubert 20
Return of Dr. Fu Manchu, The (novel) 33, 59
Return of Fu Manchu, The (proposed film) 49
Reynolds, Betty 29
Rhode, John 43
Rice, Craig 73
Richmond, John 47
Ridley, Arnold 44

Robey, George 72
Rogers, Roc 73, 74
Rohmer Review, The (magazine) 47, 60
Rohmer, Elizabeth Sax 5, 24, 37, 47
Rohmer, Sax 1-10, 12, 14-21, 23-26, 28, 31-33, 36-40, 45-49, 66-73
Romance of Sorcery, The (novel) 7
Rose, Howard 68
Round in Fifty (stage play) 72

Salomonson, Terry 6
Samson, Ivan 68
Sarnoff, Robert 72
Sax Rohmer Presents (proposed series) 72
Scarlet Street (magazine) 59
Schadow, Karl 6
Scott, Harold 68
Screentest (radio program) 74
Secombe, Harry 72
Secret Egypt (stage play) 39, 69
Sellers, Peter 72
Seven Sins (novel) 48
Seymour, Dan 74
Shadow of Fu Manchu, The (comic strip) 65
Shadow of Fu Manchu, The (radio program) 29, 37, 49-65, 71
Shadow of Sumuru, The (radio program) 69-70
Shadwell, Charles 45
Shelley, Norman 43, 44
Sherlock Holmes (radio program) 1, 29
Show People (radio program) 72
Siegel, David 6
Simpson, Ronald 68
Sins of Sumuru, The (novel) 69
Snowden, Eric 51

Stafford, Hanley 49
Stamford, John 31, 51
Stanich, Ray 60
Starita, Rudy 45
Stella Dallas (radio program) 20
Striker, Fran 35
Stringer, Lewis 69
Sturgis, Gloria 74
Suspense (radio program) 30
Swope, Jr., Herbert Bayard 71

Tales of the Foreign Legion (radio program) 28, 29, 31
Tales of the Texas Rangers (television program) 72
Taylor, Davidson 24
Ten Minute Alibi, The (novel) 44
Tennyson, Alfred 36
Terry and the Pirates (comic strip) 19, 47
This Week (magazine) 46, 47
Thompson, Bob 49
Thompson, J. Walter 42
Three Wise Fools (stage play) 29
Titheradge, Pamela 40
Train, Jack 45
Trent, William 68
Trial of Fu Manchu, The (novel) 59
Truman, Ralph 68, 69
Trumbull, Steve 24

Urquhart, Charley 54

Van Ash, Cay 5, 6, 37, 39, 40, 47
Variety (periodical) 24, 42, 43, 71, 73

Waldman, Ronald 43
Walker, Rani 39
Walker, Stuart 13
Wallace, Edgar 15
Waller, Rani 40

Warburton, Charles 23, 24, 29, 51
Warner Lester, Manhunter (radio program) 35, 36
Wattis, Richard 44, 45, 69
Webb, Dr. Joe 6
What Happened at 8:20? (radio program) 43
What's My Line? (television program) 29
Wheatley, Alan 68
White Velvet (novel) 66-69
White, Bob 29, 51
Williams, Bransby 36
Wilson, Norman 52
Wilson, Willeen 44
Winslow, Paule 51
Wong, Anna May 4
Woodburn, James 47
Woods, A.H. 7
Woolrich, Cornell 73
Wright, Paul 14
Wylie, Julian 72
Wylie, Laurie 72
Wynn, Ed 35

Yates, Hal 45
Yellow Claw, The (cliffhanger) 9, 47
Yellow Danger, The (novel) 2
Yellow Peril, The (book) 6
Yellow Shadows (novel) 9, 10
Young, Arthur 39, 41, 69
Yu'an Hee See Laughs (novel) 19, 20
Yu'an Hee See Laughs (radio program) 19, 20

About the Author

DUBBED AS THE "YOUNG ISAAC ASIMOV" by Ivan Shreve of *Thrilling Days of Yesteryear*, Martin Grams, Jr. has authored or co-authored over thirty books about old-time radio and retro television, and hundreds of magazine articles for such periodicals as *Radio Recall, Scarlet Street, Filmfax,* and SPERDVACs *Radiogram*. Among his accomplishments are books documenting the history of *The Time Tunnel, Renfrew of the Mounted, The Shadow, Truth or Consequences* and *'Way Out*. His highly-acclaimed book titled *The Twilight Zone: Unlocking the Door to a Television Classic* won the 2008 Rondo Award for "Best Book of the Year."

Martin is the recipient of the 1999 Ray Stanich Award, the 2005 Parley E. Baer Award and the 2005 Stone/Waterman Award. Both Martin and Terry co-wrote *The Green Hornet: A History of Radio, Motion Pictures, Comics and Television* (2010), based on another radio property to originate from radio station WXYZ.

'WAY OUT: A History and Episode Guide to Roald Dahl's Spooky 1961 Television Program

In the spring of 1961, CBS premiered a short-lived television program hosted by author Roald Dahl, titled *Way Out*. The creepy late-night horror program aired right before *The Twilight Zone*, but spun a gruesome tale of horror for horror's sake. This book documents the entire history of the program, what specifically led to the creation and the details regarding why the program went off the air after 14 episodes. Scans of archival documents (one reprinted below as an example), photographs and production files are reprinted, along with plot summaries for episodes that never went before the cameras.

THE GREEN HORNET: A History of Radio, Motion Pictures, Comics and Television

A complete history of the radio series from the creation to conception sketches, reprints from production files to the untold adventures, biographic details of the cast and the characters they played and background information is all provided under one cover. Also included are details of the two cliffhanger serials produced by Universal in the early forties, the unaired 1952 television pilot, the long-running popularity of the comic books and the William Dozier television series (1966-67). A complete episode guide documents every adventure including unproduced scripts and plot ideas.

THE SHADOW: The History and Mystery of the Radio Program, 1930-1954

"For those who first heard *The Shadow* on the air when radio was young, this book will bring back memories. For those too young to remember the radio show, this is a wonderful introduction. For the collector and historian of old-time radio, there are facts here they may be seeing for the first time. For everyone else, this is a book to treasure."

J. Randolph Cox
Editor, *Dime Novel Round-Up*

THE TOP 100 CLASSIC RADIO SHOWS

A compendium of the top radio shows from the golden age of Hollywood. This book is chock-full of fascinating facts and behind-the-scenes information about the best shows from every era including the 1930s, '40s, and '50s. Organized into six categories, you'll learn tantalizing tidbits about the shows and talent who made them famous. Includes comedies, westerns, dramas, variety shows, mysteries and suspense, sci-fi and superheroes. Settle into your easy chair and get ready to revisit the golden oldies, including *The Roy Rogers Show*, *The War of the Worlds*, *The Bob Hope Show*, *The Shadow*, and much more. Includes three audio CDs featuring one radio show from each genre.

THE TWILIGHT ZONE: Unlocking the Doors to a Television Classic

"Readers who feel they've entered this dimension before, namely via Marc Scott Zicree's *Twilight Zone Companion* years ago, are in for a treat. Grams has dug further than any other researcher into this durable anthology's creation and history, a series which included amongs its fans novelist Ayn Rand and actress Jodie Foster... *The Twilight Zone: Unlocking the Door to a Television Classic* is a proud testament to the series's enduring appeal."

Mark Phillips,
book review issue #120
of *Filmfax*

"I'm blown away by the mass of data... by the attention to the smallest detail. You deserve the highest praise for this book. It puts everything else written about *Twilight Zone* in the shade. Monumental and fascinating, and hugely informative!"

Science-Fiction author
William F. Nolan

"The word DEFINITIVE is not one that should be bandied about loosely or bestowed too readily on any text. However, Martin Grams Jr.'s newest television history can, without reservation, be called definitive, essential, benchmark, and all other terms that indicate no collection should be without it."

Tony Fonseca,
Dead Reckonings, Spring 2009

RENFREW OF THE MOUNTED: A History of Laurie York Erskine's Canadian Mountie Franchise

There can be no debate that Laurie York Erskine's greatest success was *Renfrew of the Mounted*, the dramatic series of a Canadian Mountie who was more than a match for the wiliest and most hard-boiled of criminals. The cry known as the Renfrew call—which children all over America imitated, heard daily on the long-running radio program—echoed through city streets and alleys. In an era when brutality and bloodshed seemed to be exerting a baleful influence on young and old, Renfrew was unusual in that he dealt with his enemies without stooping to torture, dishonesty, and third-degree methods. In consequence, a greater strain was put on his courage and moral behavior, and he was respected, even revered, by the underworld. At the peak of his popularity, the followers of Erskine's stories, books, and radio programs could be counted in the millions.

THE LONE RANGER: The Early Years, 1933–1937

By Terry Salomonson and Martin Grams, Jr.

When *The Lone Ranger* premiered on the evening of January 31, 1933, no one involved with the creation of the program suspected that "Hi-Yo, Silver!" would become an expression that would enter America's lexicon. For more than two decades, radio listeners were treated to the adventures of the "masked rider of the plains," who rode a fiery horse across the length of seven western states in pursuit of lawbreakers. With the assistance of Tonto, his faithful Indian companion, The Lone Ranger exchanged fisticuffs with outlaws who preyed upon the meek. The Lone Ranger quickly became mythic to juvenile listeners who faithfully tuned in to the radio program three nights a week.

Regrettably, it was not until 1938 that the radio broadcasts were recorded on a regular basis. Consequently, very little has been documented about those first five years, herein referred to as "The Early Years." Historians Terry Salomonson and Martin Grams have combined three decades of research to present the facts behind the origin of *The Lone Ranger*, and the ongoing development both artistic and commercial, along with scans of archival documents to back up the facts. In addition, this book offers plot summaries for pre-1938 radio broadcasts, filling a void that was sorely needed. Did you know The Lone Ranger and Tonto had a juvenile sidekick named Little Davy? Did you know our heroes had a canine companion? Did you know Tonto was once engaged? This definitive history presents a portrait of both the beloved characters and their dramatic adventures that fans of *The Lone Ranger* will enjoy reading.

www.ingramcontent.com/pod-product-compliance
Lightning Source LLC
Chambersburg PA
CBHW071625170426
43195CB00038B/2120